D0226204

William Fawcett Hill's
LEARNING THROUGH
DISCUSSION
Third Edition

This book is dedicated to William Fawcett Hill, author of the first editions of *Learning Through Discussion*. Bill pioneered this method of learning, in part prompted by his intimate knowledge of the workings of small groups. I would also like to thank Ronald K. Lippitt and Marc Chesler, who taught me about democracy in the classroom, and Paula Freire, who taught me about the destructiveness of contemporary education. Herb Kohl, John Holt, A. S. Neill, Sylvia Warner, and Jill Weston are all teachers who have shown me better ways to be with younger students and inspired me to think about better ways to be with young adults. Albert Elias first introduced me to the power of groups. My colleagues who enrich my group life at UCLA include Robert Emerson, Michael Goldstein, David Lopez, Melvin Pollner, and Michael Newcomb. Finally, there is my wife, Roslyn, who supports my teaching by living a life of the web, a metaphor that she used even before Carol Gilligan wrote her pioneering work. Michelle Charness, Johanna Kipperman, and Susan Vasile would like to dedicate this book to family members and friends who supported their work.

—Jerry Rabow

William Fawcett Hill's

LEARNING THROUGH DISCUSSION

Third Edition

Jerome Rabow
Michelle A. Charness
Johanna Kipperman
Susan Radcliffe-Vasile

WAVELAND

PRESS, INC.

Long Grove, Illinois

For information about this book, contact:
Waveland Press, Inc.
4180 IL Route 83, Suite 101
Long Grove, IL 60047-9580
(847) 634-0081
info@waveland.com
www.waveland.com

Cover photos: Shasta Britt Phillips

Copyright © 1994 by Jerome Rabow
Reissued 2000 by Waveland Press, Inc.

10-digit ISBN 1-57766-111-7
13-digit ISBN 978-1-57766-111-5

All rights reserved. No part of this book may be reproduced, stored in a retrieval system, or transmitted in any form or by any means without permission in writing from the publisher.

Printed in the United States of America

11   10   9

Contents

Acknowledgments

I have been experimenting with variants of this discussion method for over 15 years and thus I am unable to thank all the many students at UCLA who have contributed to this discussion guide. The following students, however, can be cited for their contributions to this project: Peggy DeDiego, Sandra Leal, Shari Levey, Shari Meisler, Amanda Tellez, Michael Wharton, Jina Yoon, Jackie Chavez, Romi Weinhouse, Lindy Wolf, Gloria Martinez, Jennifer Ferris, Daryl El Mouchi, Kelly Wochick, Cason Lee, Jami Kerr, Leann Chen, Brittany Walker, Julia Helm, Michael Murphy, Ronald Nunan, Jodi Deming, Lara Saunders, Angela Buenning, Jana Bartke, Sydelle A. Fisher, Giselle Boras, Roxanne Copeland, Lynn Sappington, Leah Mintz, Jody Islas, Yvonne S. Lee, Susan Moriarty, Lara Pourgtian, Carmela Lomonaco, David Shimuzi, Chandler Rand, Leslie Thinnes, Sharmen Taylor, Paul Moore, and Patrick Goodman. Debra de Causin and Marilyn Duncan were especially helpful and supportive of the LTD method. Students at the California Graduate Institute who were particularly insightful were Toby Salter, Carolyn Roberts, Sheila Cohen, and Jill Barth. Jennifer Choe and Judy Lee did a final proofing and editing.

Foreword

Thirty years after the wars on the merits of group discussion versus lecture, a new version of Learning Through Discussion (LTD) appears. A discerning consumer of books should ask, "Who needs it?" "Does it differ in a substantial way from the original product?" and "If we were indifferent before why should we now feel differently?" In this Foreword I shall attempt to answer these seemingly impertinent questions.

At the outset, let me identify with the aggressors and admit that if we really believed in conservation of the environment we would try to save the trees by the simple expedient of reducing by half the quantity of books published in any given year. It is believed that this would not really have any deleterious effect on the national IQ although the savings in trees might be used up in the subsequent Civil Rights debate.

A hiatus of thirty years since the first Sage publication of LTD suggests that the author of LTD felt no urgency for a follow-up. However, this original author now feels that the time has come to revisit and revise LTD.

Why?

It has become apparent that there has been a considerable audience for LTD since its first appearance thirty years ago and sales have not decreased significantly over this span. Nor have they increased! According to the publisher and the authors of this edition the original was not "user-friendly." Mea cupla. Fortunately, when the book was first conceived in the good old days, the concept, with all its CC (Consumer Correctness) was not in the academic lexicon. To reach the light of day, this version of LTD is meant to be more user-friendly.

Also the book was used by instructors and teachers of widely divergent groups. Many a loyal practitioner has taken me aside to confide that they have liked the overall design but found it expedient to tamper with certain features. The earnestness of these true believers was touching and I invariably countered with a somewhat Einsteinian explanation that the original LTD book put forth a General Theory of Learning Through Discussion and that each circumstance requires a Special Theory. This new version addresses this matter very satisfactorily and is designed, in a user-friendly fashion, specifically for use in college and university classrooms. This is its main strength and its justification. If you are running or participating in a college-level course and are considering incorporating discussion groups into your pedagogy, then this is the book for you.

Taking advantage of the opportunity to write a Foreword and thus breaking thirty years of silence, the author insists on sharing some further LTD insights gathered over these three decades.

The variance in behavior from group to group can be largely accounted for by four factors. Let us examine these four factors and some of their implications for LTD groups.

1. Group Leadership. It is often said that the group is an extension of the leader's ego. Therefore some instructors are more likely than others to enjoy success with discussion groups. Nonetheless, if the instructor is to have a successful experience, he must stand four square behind the LTD method. He or she must not allow the group to become something akin to a singles bar nor resemble a debating society. All of the failures—not many I hasten to add—that have come to my attention can be attributed to a reluctance on the part of the instructor to implement and maintain LTD procedures.

Because of the pervasive effect of the leader, no one member should emerge as the leader in an LTD discussion group and the facilitator should insist on the formal leadership being rotated. No one should be designated driver for every session.

2. Group Composition. It is self-evident that changes in membership in a group changes the style of the operation of the group. Thus some thought should be given to manipulating the composition of LTD groups if the situation allows this.

In actual practice it is unavoidable not to get highly motivated and group-oriented students in the same class with shy, silent, and poorly motivated students. Research indicates that if these kinds of students are well distributed among the groups in a given class then the resulting discussions will be salutary.

3. Group Development. It has been observed that groups establish their own *modus operandi* early in their existence and show little or no propensity to change. LTD is designed to support the development of the group. However, in modern education, classes form and reform after every quarter or semester and thus there is no continuity in the developmental life of a classroom study group. Limited experience supports the notion that the efficacy of a learning group would improve as the group is given the opportunity to develop. The shelf life of a group in academia is so brief that typically half its time is spent in learning the LTD method and half in learning the material. It is only logical to expect greater things from a discussion group that meets regularly for the whole academic year.

4. Context. Just within the college or university setting there are contextual differences. Some meetings are conducted in chairs encircled in a classroom, others around a table, and still others in deeply carpeted conference rooms. The site and physical facilities are obviously contextual variables, but there are a host of other contextual variables that have outcome effects that are not so obvious. Examples are institutional and social mores and rules, grading practices, and availability of a suitable text. A group leader needs to be aware of these contextual variables and to use them effectively or compensate for them.

Within a historical perspective, the original LTD was ahead of its time. This is because it was formulated within a cognitive paradigm before the so-called "cognitive revolution" occurred in the social sciences. The present authors have chosen not to use the "Group Cognitive Map" terminology of the original LTD but they have retained the cognitive structure and idealogy consonant with this terminology. These authors mention some of the research that has been done on LTD and clearly make the case for more research being needed to optimize the method. The cognitive paradigm suggests new avenues and explanatory concepts for this type of research. For example, we might invoke Craik & Lockhart's (1972) "deep processing" as an explanatory concept for the enhanced learning and retention in discussion groups.

One final observation. It has often been said that a group is a microcosm of society. The fact is that the group is the crucible in which democratic principles and practices are forged and that both the student and instructor can learn about what makes democracy work and about the threats to its existence. This has been for me the hidden agenda sustaining my efforts through the years with LTD.

William Fawcett Hill

Introduction:
The Goals and Opportunities
of Discussion Groups

Learning Through Discussion is a new edition of Dr. William Hill's highly successful book that introduced this unique discussion process. As such, throughout the book we have incorporated Dr. Hill's original words and ideas for a successful group discussion. After all, this is a description of his model, and that model works—as much today as when the first edition was published in 1962.

So in what ways is this edition new? The primary reason for writing a new edition was to make *Learning Through Discussion* more relevant for today's students. We have added examples from real classes and real students, with pertinent suggestions for conducting Learning Through Discussion (LTD) groups that are based upon years of leading and supporting such groups. We have expanded the explanation of the process by adding suggestions on how to get started and covering application of the topics discussed to other materials and to the self in more detail. Because so many students these days are alienated from the learning process, we have placed emphasis on these steps.

In addition, we describe behaviors that are nonfunctional in LTD groups, listening skills necessary to the group performance, and the relationship of LTD to the cognitive domain. We have elaborated upon the role of the leader and the instructor, both essential to the success of LTD. Finally, we have added a detailed discussion of grading. Unfortunately, it is impossible to get away from the fact that grading is a necessity in today's academic arena, something that neither students nor instructors can choose to ignore. Thus we have included guidelines for methods of grading using the LTD method.

In the following chapters, we will describe the process of Learning Through Discussion in detail. In the first chapter, "A New Method of Studying," we examine the relationships between students and the learning process and point out the difference between how students usually study and how students must prepare in order to participate in a LTD group. After all, even though LTD has been used in classrooms for a number of years, it means an entirely new method of learning and studying for most students. We also briefly cover what makes a good group in this chapter.

In Chapter 2, "The Learning Through Discussion Process Plan," we introduce the eight-step process plan, the procedure by which the course material is discussed adequately and learning takes place. These steps are: Checking In, Vocabulary, General Statement of Author's Message, Identification and Discussion of Major Themes and Subtopics, Application of Material to Other Works, Application of Material to the Self, Evaluation of the Author's Presentation, and Evaluation of the Group and Individual Performance.

In Chapter 3, "Criteria for Initiation of Learning Through Discussion," we look more closely at what makes a good group in terms of interpersonal expectations. These group expectations must include regular attendance, cooperative learning, active participation, adequate coverage of material, and constructive evaluation. In addition, the importance of speculative and confrontive statements is discussed.

In Chapter 4, "Group Members' Roles and Skills," we distinguish the difference between productive and nonproductive behavior and discuss group maintenance roles and task roles group members must enact for the group to be successful. For example, student members must be willing to confront the errors of fellow group members, to clarify and summarize what has been discussed thus far, and to evaluate the progress of the group and the individual members. To fulfill these roles, students must come to class ready to participate. We therefore offer an outline on how to prepare for class.

In Chapter 5, "Role of the Leader," we describe the role of the student leader in terms of the added responsibilities of time and commitment as well as some of the specific job requirements. Obviously, the role of the professor is crucial for the ultimate success of LTD.

In Chapter 6 we give the instructor some suggestions for implementing the LTD method, gleaned from our many years of experience.

Readers will also want to look over some of the materials presented in the Appendix. Students will find the list of skills useful for classroom discussion invaluable. A variety of supporting materials are also included—examples of a grade sheet, postmeeting reaction sheet, and an evaluation form. Each of these may be copied and used in the course or may be changed to fit the needs of the individual groups. Finally, some of the research that supports group discussion learning is presented.

We wrote this book to bring Dr. Hill's method to an entirely new generation of students. It is our hope that students and instructors will utilize the method in their classes and so discover Dr. Hill's exciting world in which learning is a stimulating, fulfilling endeavor and in which students can take charge of their learning.

1 A New Method of Studying

Learning Through Discussion (LTD) is both absorbing and exciting, but it also requires more work than the typical lecture or lecture-discussion class. To suggest anything contrary would be to set the student up for disappointment and potential failure. Not everyone welcomes the intellectual challenge and interpersonal stimulation that discussion group dynamics offers. By precisely identifying what the LTD method involves in terms of student preparation as well as participation, leaders will help students become familiar with the demands of group contribution.

Certainly this method doesn't allow students to remain passive about learning; it requires active involvement in the acquisition and development of knowledge. The discussion process moves away from the realm of lecturing—a realm in which students too often merely memorize and regurgitate ready-made facts. In striking contrast, LTD dynamics facilitates a high level of analytical thinking along with the opportunity to evaluate one's own intellectual and interpersonal abilities. While the students are learning the subject matter, they also will be mastering critical-thinking skills that will stand them in good stead through college and throughout life—skills that are especially important in today's work circumstances in which workers can anticipate changing jobs (and careers) several times.

Directing one's own level of learning as well as that of one's peers —whether it be intellectual or socioemotional development—is stimulating. Students may even find themselves enjoying learning! For example, one sophomore noted on his last day of his LTD group:

> I've always been able to get pretty O.K. grades because I can cram like crazy. I know how to cram and I've done it often enough that I know what to do and I can always do O.K. But I never remember the stuff after finals. I do remember the stuff we talked about in here. Most of the articles are real for me. Maybe it's because I read them and then had to talk about them, but it also seems like they're connected to people in this group and to me. And somehow the books all have greater meaning because I've heard us all talk about them, and it's been fun. I'm amazed that I have been able to learn from you guys.

Here is a young man who has discovered the difference between cramming for an exam and really learning the course material. When cramming, he would forget the subject almost immediately after the final exam. But here the subject was made relevant to him and therefore remembered.

Learning and Studying

Before dealing with the nuts and bolts of the discussion method, let's examine the relationship between the student and the learning process in order to evaluate what is required of the discussion group so that it may support the learning process. How does the average college classroom facilitate learning? Well, students usually learn the course material and pass the examinations by simply completing homework and classroom assignments. Like the sophomore above, most students can pass an exam by cramming the material related to the test. If they regularly attend lectures, study, and memorize, there should be no problem! If there were, the student would attend a seminar that gives tips on learning how to study.

Although these types of study habits are sufficient for most college courses, they really don't encourage learning. How much, for example, can students remember from their Introduction to Earth Sciences lectures even the following semester? Or their history class? For example, one student recently complained of a Roman History course she had taken in which the instructor came into the room, placed her notes on the podium, read her lecture to the class, and then immediately left, rarely even looking at the students. When asked about what she had learned, the student admitted that she could remember very little of anything—even though she had received an A in the course. But when asked about a 20th-century American History course she had taken 2 years earlier, this same student enthusiastically began to enumerate some of the issues and ideas raised in the class. Why did she remember? We suggest that it was primarily because of the discussion format. Even though the course did not specifically use LTD, the instructor encouraged his students to think by asking—and having the students answer—questions that made the material relevant to them. In so doing, he got them involved in the learning process.

Studying for LTD Groups

How one learns about a subject in the lecture situation is self-evident, but how anyone learns in the discussion group is a bit of a mystery to most students. The LTD method requires a specific type of homework and a different study technique. Listen to how one student prepared for his second class discussion:

> I had to begin by being prepared for the next meeting. . . . This meant doing the reading. It was Tuesday night, only the second day of school, and I was doing the reading for the next class meeting on Thursday. My roommates were puzzled by my actions. "Are you feeling O.K.?" they asked in mock concern. I was a little unsure myself. Yet, I came prepared for class that Thursday having read and taken notes on the article. I did prove myself to the others on that day and the days that followed, but maybe most important, I proved to myself that I could do it. The kind of preparation that I did that night became common; in fact, it actually increased as the class progressed. It often wouldn't be enough to read through an article once for the purposes of discussion, so I would read it again.

This student is on his way to becoming an effective discussion participant. He knows the material and is prepared to *say* something about it. This means thinking about and anticipating his contribution, something that cannot be postponed to the hour just before the class meeting. Not only must the preparation be done in advance of each and every discussion period, but the method also makes special and unique homework demands, which will be covered in detail later in this book.

At this stage some students may already be saying: "New type of study habits? Extra homework? Forget it!" "How can a fellow student teach me? I'd probably do better with my T.A. or the Prof." Based on our experience, we believe this method will help students to develop a range of skills (verbal, analytical, and interpersonal) that will last long beyond the immediate task. We also believe it will increase their understanding of course material (see the Appendix for some of the research on this subject). But the bottom line is our belief that this method engenders critical thinking, higher levels of learning, and more personal satisfaction when compared to lectures.

How is this done? Students often have a great verbal facility and are able to refer to various concepts and issues. Yet these same students, as a result of the traditional methods of learning, lack any real, personal understanding of the basic facts, their implications or their connections to other materials and to the students' own lives.

LTD attempts to remedy such problems. As we shall see in the Group Process Plan, discussed in the next chapter, strong emphasis is placed on learning precisely what the author has to say on a subject. It also requires students to formulate and verbalize their own understanding as well as to clarify any misinterpretations or confusions other students may introduce. All this can lead to real learning, rather than the parrot-like regurgitation of memorized information.

By helping one another to understand, students are teaching and learning to communicate ideas, both their own and others'. Even if they are equally competent, there will always be students who do not understand some aspect of the material. The LTD method encourages students to teach and help clarify issues. Because students approach the same material from different vantage points, more often than not, some members will be able to clarify or diagnose the nature of the difficulty through discussion. Often, students can recognize difficulties quicker than the instructor because they approach the new material from a fresh viewpoint. Instructors are often so immersed in the subject that it may seem impossible for them to understand the problems the students are having with the material. Thus we believe that although groups can at times reinforce pluralistic ignorance or engage in "group-think," when done properly, LTD can convert blind spots and misunderstandings into opportunities for students to learn and teach.

A Democratic Group Discussion Model

The LTD method depends expressly on the use of democratic dynamics in contrast to groups modeled on the authoritarian style or the laissez-faire mode. In an authoritarian group, the leader, or the authority, makes demands on the group, leading the discussion in the direction he or she believes most constructive. This method may induce group cohesiveness, but fails to take advantage of the group dynamics that generate new potential for learning. At the same time, democratic principles should not be confused with the laissez-faire method in which anything goes. Anything and everything may be perfectly acceptable for therapy or consciousness-raising groups, but where didactic material must be mastered, there must be some method of proceeding. Any random comment is definitely not appropriate grist for the mill, nor is the development of a "good group" more important than mastery of the subject matter. Something other than free association by the whole group or domination by one member is required.

Thus, discussion participants should promote equality in communication; each member's freedom to participate should be subject only to the group's allotment of time and task achievement. Because principles of the democratic communication style tend to vary, no discussion group is ever a replica of another; however, this mode is most commonly achieved when the participants' commitment to learning is primary. Such a commitment empowers group members with a unique desire to teach as well as to acquire new perspectives related to theoretical and self-applications. Individual members of such groups tend to pay particular attention to their own development and to the development of their peers, accepting the dynamics of the group, but also analyzing how to improve the level of learning and the overall cohesiveness of the group.

A Good Group

What, then, constitutes a good group? The development of a "good group" and the learning process of the individual student are one and the same. A good group handles the problems that arise and realizes the potential of the members in order to enhance learning. Beyond that, each group evolves properties and strengths of its own that encourage learning.

A good group should also promote a warm, friendly atmosphere that encourages all members to participate. Even though realistically not all members participate and interact equally, all must participate from time to time. Finally, students cooperate to master the subject matter. The LTD method facilitates the development of such a group.

The Learning Through Discussion method consists of three parts, each essential to its success:

Part I: *LTD Process Plan:* Eight steps make up the LTD method of discussion. These steps are the cognitive map that will be used by discussants. Each step has its own rationale and unique goal.

Part II: *List of Criteria for Initiation of LTD:* These are the informal expectations that accompany excellent discussions. Whereas the eight process steps are the formal requirement, these expectations describe the values that participants are expected to develop.

Part III: *Group Members' Roles and Skills:* Members must develop certain skills and roles if their LTD group is to be productive. These skills and roles legitimize and justify the enactment of selective behavior by group members.

Let us first look at the LTD Process Plan.

2 The Learning Through Discussion Process Plan

As already indicated, group discussions are often characterized by lack of direction. Topics that are discussed arise either haphazardly or at the insistence of a dominating member. No one knows what behavior is appropriate. In reality, appropriate behavior consists of developing some procedure for adequately discussing and ultimately learning the material. The LTD Process Plan is a procedural tool that outlines an orderly sequence that a group should follow in order to learn from discussion.

The LTD Process Plan is made up of eight steps, which are listed in Table 2.1. These are the nuts and bolts of Learning Through Discussion and must be mastered and understood in order for group discussions to be effective and satisfying. The most common complaint of discussion group members is that the group never covers the material, spending too much time on one aspect to the detriment of all the rest or getting sidetracked to other topics. To avoid this difficulty, time must be budgeted and allocated wisely, and the discussion conducted accordingly. Each step presented below has a corresponding time allotment. Although the suggested allotment can vary according to the particular discussion needs of a specific group, successful groups have followed these suggestions closely and achieved wonderful results.

Table 2.1 Eight-Step LTD Group Process Plan

Step 1	Checking in	2-4 minutes
Step 2	Vocabulary	3-4 minutes
Step 3	General statement of author's message	5-6 minutes
Step 4	Identification and discussion of major themes or subtopics	10-12 minutes
Step 5	Application of material to other works	15-16 minutes
Step 6	Application of material to self	10-12 minutes
Step 7	Evaluation of author's presentation	3-4 minutes
Step 8	Evaluation of group and individual performance	7-8 minutes
	Total Time	60 minutes

Our experience is that the total time of 60 minutes is ideal. Some college classes meet for 2 hours, so 60-70 minutes can be allotted. This can be modified according to the time allocated for discussion, however. For example, in some courses in which vocabulary is important, Step 2 may take up a much greater portion of available time. In a literature course, discussion of the themes may take an entire class period.

Let us look at these steps in more detail.

Step 1: Checking In

During the first meeting every group member must get to know other members by first names. One way to do this is to ask each one to repeat the names of all the other members. Another recommended icebreaker is for each student to interview another member of the group and then introduce that member to the whole circle. We also suggest that group members exchange phone numbers. This will help if a student misses a discussion or wants to go over a point in preparation for, or subsequent to, a discussion.

During the second, third, and fourth meetings, groups often have trouble getting started. Apparently, each member is waiting for someone else to get the group going. Checking in can serve as an icebreaker, allowing students the opportunity to greet one another and express feelings related to the group discussion. This in turn will help to establish an environment of warmth and concern for what everyone thinks and has to say. At this stage some students may indicate whether or not they feel competent to discuss that day's material, or that they are having a great or lousy day. Some comments that illustrate this step are:

- I'm real eager to get started today; I've got something really exciting to contribute.
- Not me! I'm tired. I wrote a paper till 3 a.m.
- I'm burnt out today, and I'm not prepared.

Students need to disclose such feelings at the start of the session instead of trying to deal with them during the process of the group discussion. Checking in provides a bridge for students to talk about ideas, but it needs to be done quickly! There is always the danger that it will eat up a lot of time, especially in colleges where people are stressed out and alienated from one another and are therefore eager to talk with fellow students and hear about their similar problems, experiences, and situations.

CASE STUDY

At the first meeting of an introductory sociology class, after introducing the organization of the class, grading, and exams, the instructor divides the class into 10 discussion groups, each with six students. He then asks the students to introduce themselves by giving their name, major, college year, why they are taking the course, and what they expect to get out of it. The instructor also suggests that students exchange phone numbers with other group members and asks the students to show that they know everyone's name before the class is dismissed.

In most groups this is done by having students introduce themselves and everyone previously introduced. The instructor then assigns the book *Learning Through Discussion* and the first chapter of the text for the next class period.

In general, it is beneficial for students to devote one class period to using the LTD group to discuss LTD. Everyone then is starting with the same expectations. However, if time is short, as in summer school or with the quarter system, the first LTD could be on the first reading assignment. Sometimes the instructor can do an LTD with the entire class on the first day to illustrate the method. This works well with something all have read or seen, such as a movie. The instructor may also wish to show the video on LTD that is available to further illustrate the LTD method.

Step 2: Vocabulary

When reading difficult material, looking words up in the dictionary is helpful, even for students who think they know the definition. The act of defining terms in itself constitutes learning. This step allows the student to share creatively the acquisition of new vocabulary. Students may want to design their own presentation of new words, but whatever they do, it should be fun. For example, one student may create a word game, like trying to guess the correct context in which to use a particular word. This is an example of one student's effort to teach his peers:

> The word *cogent* means:
> 1. a cleaning agent
> 2. disinterested
> 3. forcible
> 4. convincing
> 5. a men's bathroom, with two urinals
> 6. both 3 and 4

At first glance, the vocabulary stage is deceiving in its simplistic appearance, but in addition to enhancing the students' command of the English language, vocabulary utilization checks the functioning and dynamics of the group. For example, if group members consistently admit that they are unable to keep up with their assigned weekly reading, this suggests a lack of commitment to the method and their group. Participants who are actively reading and questioning complex vocabulary words are usually members of a discussion group in which a sense of unity and higher learning remains primary.

This step does not require a maximum or minimum number of words discussed, leaving the group an opportunity to test group members' level of reading as well as group dynamics. A rule of thumb is that the focus should be not on who knows the words (e.g., who has looked them up) but on who doesn't. Students will learn not just about words, but also something about their own reading style, interest in language, and the study habits of others. In addition, this often teaches another, more constructive way of reading.

One last caution. *Webster's Collegiate Dictionary* is not necessarily the best source of information; in scientific and technical courses, students may need specialized dictionaries, which the instructor must make sure are available.

CASE STUDY

While reading the assigned chapters in *The White Hotel* for his class in psychoanalytic sociology, Collin came across *lugubrious*, a word he had heard numerous times and believed he under-stood. He proceeded to look the word up in the dictionary and was shocked. In the class discussion, he decided to tell his LTD group that he had always thought the word meant "oily." A few students laughed until Cindy admitted that she had thought the word meant "stupid." The LTD leader then asked the students to use the word correctly in a sentence.

(NOTE: Students who have just read this little case study without looking up the word lugubrious will need to change the way they read.)

Step 3: General Statement of the Author's Message

The purpose of this step is to obtain a grasp of the overall meaning of the assigned reading. Verbal expressions of the general state-ment help to zero in on the topic for discussion. Some authors, particularly of textbooks, begin each chapter with a clearly defined general statement, which greatly simplifies the task and cuts down the time spent in this step. If the reading assignment is the report of an experiment, the general hypothesis of the researcher can often serve as a clear general statement. In many cases, however, such a statement of the author's purpose may be difficult and require much thought.

Even where general statements can be found in "title" headings, students should state them in their own words. Likewise, if students accurately verbalize a statement, other members should restate it in their own words. By restating what another has said, members provide feedback to the original speaker and to others of their understanding and commitment. Enunciating the author's purpose for writing an article or book concisely and thoughtfully underscores the author's main point and launches the group into the discussion.

CASE STUDY

Course: Social Psychology
Assignment: Codification of Reality: Lineal and Nonlineal
by Dorothy Lee

Daryl: I think the author says that all reality is personal . . . like it's subjective.

Pat: I think the subjective part is true, but it's only one aspect of what I got out of the article. Because I think the author is also saying that reality is out there. . . . It's real. It can be measured. It can be evaluated, and therefore it's real.

Candy: Maybe you're both right. . . . The stuff that's out there is real because we believe it to be real. So that means that it is not only out there but that we can decide and discover what is out there, often when we may not see or feel it.

Step 4: Identification and Discussion of Major Themes or Subtopics

Reading materials can be broken down into a number of important themes or subtopics. In many course textbooks the author or editor provides an overview of the main topics in each section and usually supplies subheadings. In other text-oriented books, the author's purpose may also be gleaned from the expanded table of contents. If this is the case, students need to restate the general purpose of the assignment in their own words; in so doing, they discover whether they do indeed understand that purpose and also launch the group discussion. Quite often, the task may be more difficult, as in a literature course in which the whole novel or short story must be examined to determine the theme or themes of the work. Certainly, the themes of Shakespeare's *Hamlet* or Joyce's *Dubliners* cannot be explicated without serious thought.

The author's work can be highlighted analytically by breaking down the major themes and connecting logic. For the sake of time management, a discussion group should identify no more than three or four topics. When more than four themes exist, the group may have to decide which are most significant. Time is an important resource that needs to be managed, and the group should not spend all its time discussing and arguing about what an author has said.

Nevertheless, although LTD emphasizes time management, if in fact the thematic step demands more concentration, time allotments can be made. When addressing themes pertaining to concise and terse articles, the themes can be generally handled within the LTD time limits. On the other hand, novels may require that a group extend its discussion of thematic structure to an entire 50-minute session. Thus the LTD method might be employed for a 2-week period. Time limits should not be used to hinder group learning but rather to minimize extraneous discussions and expedite the development of higher learning and a higher level of complex discussion.

One more point. The LTD method places greater emphasis on determining what the author has to say on a particular topic than on the opinions of the students. This is not because student opinions are thought to be of no significance. On the contrary, they are an important part of the discussion learning process. In our experience, however, groups never discover what the author has to say if members begin by giving their personal opinions. Individual likes and dislikes and opinions become the important issue, and what the author has to say attains only incidental importance. For example, most people have fixed opinions on evolution, psychoanalysis, and communism and yet have read little or nothing by Darwin, Freud, or Marx. Students who have seen any of the movies on the Kennedy assassination may have strong convictions related to various conspiracy theories and yet have never read any of the expert opinions on either side of the issue. In other words, when personal opinions are expressed before the author's themes are examined, real learning cannot take place. Thus, in LTD the expression of personal reactions is postponed until Step 8, after the group has discussed the text.

These first four steps have focused on the author's work. The tendency in groups is either to get bogged down in the author's ideas or to ignore them and get into personal applications and criticisms, which are the last few steps of the LTD method. It is most important for the leader and the group to recognize the importance of time and the necessity of discussing the author's work and having the group work on applying the author's ideas. Making sure that these two major components, the author and the self, are discussed is the responsibility of the leader. Leaders can keep time themselves or appoint group members to ensure that a certain number of minutes is allocated to each step. In our experience it has always been better for groups to adhere to a fairly rigid time schedule in the beginning stages of discussion. This ensures that all steps become part of the group's expectations. As groups develop and mature and become more efficient, time can be allocated more flexibly. The metaphor we like to use is that learning to follow the LTD method is much like learning the piano: You need to know the scales and chords before you can make music.

CASE STUDY

Course: Psychoanalytic Sociology
Novel: August *by Judith Rossner*

Jennifer: I think there is a lot to discuss in this novel. I don't know where to begin. I'm feeling totally overwhelmed.

Alex: As I see it, it seemed like we can divide this novel up into three major themes. There's Dawn and her character and her therapy and all the people in her life, and then there's Lulu, the shrink, and her character and all the people in her life, and then there is the relationship between the two of them.

Shiranda: I like that; it helps me.

Leader: I'm not sure we are going to be able to get through all the steps today. Can we just pick two of those themes and discuss them? Which do you think are the most important?

Jennifer: Well, I want to talk about Dawn because I'm in therapy, too, and I think my relationship with my therapist is a lot better.

Leader: Well, hold on. We are not talking about how these people relate to us just yet. Let's concentrate first on what the author is saying about them. Now, who else thinks that Dawn's relationships are important to discuss?

Step 5: Application of Material to Other Works

Critics of the educational system often complain that learning is too fragmentary and too concerned with the acquisition of isolated bits of information even though it is accepted that isolated facts are the first to be forgotten, or if not forgotten, seldom used in life situations. For example, the students were discussing the teaching of Herb Kohl, a white teacher who taught African-American fifth-grade students in Harlem:

Gloria: I always used the word *relevance* and thought it was overrated. That is, I used it and believed in it without understanding what it meant. But when I read how Kohl's kids were learning math just because of their interest in the Floyd Patterson-Sonny Liston fight, then it took on real meaning. I now see how kids' interests can be connected to what teachers feel is important to learn about.

Jackie: Yeah, it also became clear to me what Dewey was talking about when he kept stressing the importance of continuity in education.

These students realized that in relating math to a match, Kohl was making learning applicable to his students' lives. Suddenly, math was not a textbook exercise but something that was part of their daily living. Gloria and Jackie realized that this was an essential part of real learning.

To counteract the possibility that learning stays fragmented and isolated, LTD requires group members to allocate time and make a conscious effort to relate learning in the assignment to ideas and concepts acquired in previous meetings or other learning situations. Simply put, an application takes some of the main themes and subtopics of the material to be discussed and compares them to those of other relevant literature. This literature may include another assigned reading for the week, a past week's reading, or any other work, preferably one with which all group members are familiar. This allows everyone in the group to be able to evaluate the relevance of what is being said. For example, George Orwell's essay "On Shooting an Elephant" can be related to his autobiography *Burmese Days* or to more generic readings on colonialism—both British and U.S. Kronenfeld's *Controversial Issues in Health Care Policy* can be related to current journal articles or even newspaper articles about health care reform.

Over time the applications will probably derive exclusively from the group's common readings. Whether or not everyone agrees with a student's point of view is not important in the context of the application. The purpose of an application is to take the arguments of one author and either refute or support them by cross-referencing them with another expert point of view. A lucid analysis of the argument is essential. This means that a student should be able to translate the understanding of the article to the group while also showing how the article relates to other literature. What does a "good" application sound like? Consider the following:

> I can show how this laboratory field experiment conducted in Hungary can be used to understand the efforts of Herb Kohl, a schoolteacher in Harlem. The experiment in Hungary was done with nursery school children. The experimenter, Merei, wanted to see if these small groups of children had developed a culture, a way of doing their early morning play routines, and if they could be influenced to change their ways and habits. Change occurred only when a "diplomatic leader" was introduced into the group. The diplomat accepted the group's ways, its culture, and then slowly introduced minor modifications.
>
> It seems to me that Herb Kohl, a white teacher at an all-black school in Harlem, did the same thing. Kohl inspired unmotivated children by

acting precisely like Merei's diplomat! He gave them free time to let them develop ways of playing and doing things, and observed them carefully, noticing that they had developed a "culture" just like the kids of Hungary. He did not criticize, castigate, or intrude until he was a trusted and accepted member, rather than an outsider. When he achieved this position he began to introduce modifications in the games the children loved to play. He utilized their interests and concerns to introduce them to questions and knowledge that enhanced their interests. Over time, their appetites for learning soared, and he was able to break into the cycle of despair.

This application shows the linkages between the ideas of different authors. The principle developed in one setting has value and relevance for describing and understanding activities in different settings.

Step 6: Application of the Material to the Self

Ideally, a college education should be both theoretical, extending one's knowledge horizons, and concrete, illuminating one's life. Knowledge needs to be cumulative and integrated; it is most exciting when it has personal value or significance. "Self-applications" encourage students to make the discussion personal and rewarding. If the knowledge has some value to students, it can deepen or challenge their understanding of themselves, their relationships, and the collectives to which they belong (including the LTD group itself).

This is the main purpose of self-applications. When theoretical knowledge is applied in practical ways, people tend to feel personal attachment and identification to the material being discussed, enabling them to experience (in their own life) the author's point of view or challenge and modify it in some way. Here new theories are tested. An "application" of the Merei experiment involves the student recalling and describing experiences in groups where "leaders" tried to change the group. Alternatively, a student may have had experiences where he or she tried to change a group. Certainly, this is the problem for therapists who try to change family structures, for social workers who work with gangs, and for college instructors who attempt to change the culture of the classroom. The connection between analytical concepts (leadership, diplomacy, group culture) and one's own human experiences is what can make this learning process exciting for students.

CASE STUDY

For her class Patricia Smock wrote a self-application of Arlie Hochschild's *The Managed Heart* to her work experience at Disney.

Patricia: The reason that I chose the topic of persuasion from *The Managed Heart* and related it to the training program of Delta Airlines is because I went through a similar program at Disneyland. This training program is called the Disney University. I was required to attend the university to learn various aspects of company history, procedure, and philosophy. For example, Disney employees must use unique terminology, which sets Disneyland apart from other businesses. Customers are referred to as guests and everyone is a "very important person" (V.I.P.). I was not an employee but a cast member. My role in the show was to be a merchandise hostess (a fancy name for someone who sells souvenirs). I worked on stage and entertained an audience. We wore costumes, not uniforms. Disneyland has attractions, not rides.

The Disney University instilled such pride in me that I really became an enthusiastic cast member. I was willing to bend over backwards for the guests because I knew that Walt Disney would have wanted it that way. I took into consideration the fact that some guests had spent their life savings and had traveled halfway around the world to experience Disneyland. They deserved the best that I could offer. I found a lot of myself in the character of *The Managed Heart*'s stewardess trainee. The Disney University and Delta training programs are very similar in philosophy and content. Like the Delta Training Program, the Disney University employs all factors of successful persuasion. Both companies have strict guidelines, yet they instill a sense of pride among their employees. They are outstanding examples of service-oriented companies that have received the public accolades they deserve.

Susan: That is great, Pat. You reevaluated the Disney training program by a set of conceptual standards provided by a social scientist.

Collin: Yes, it helped us all understand how organizations gain commitments from employees. Because the assignment has been personalized, you can see your experience in a new light. I'll bet that you'll remember *The Managed Heart.* I know your situation will help me be able to apply it to future situations.

Susan: I think what is left out from this essay is the price you may have paid.

Leader: Should we discuss that issue now?

Collin: Yes, that is important.

Step 7: Evaluation of the Author's Presentation

In the discussion process, personal reactions are important. A particularly difficult piece of writing can be very frustrating, and students have every right to express their feelings of frustration. An effective group process allows for such critical reactions, but if learning is to be served, criticism should be constructive. As discussed earlier, the development of the ability to apply critical thinking may be more important than the learning of the material itself, as it will assist the student in future learning and life situations. Therefore, if one can rise above emotional unloading of personal gripes and one's own critical faculties, the result will be worth the effort. A little complaining may be necessary and valuable, but it should be recognized that it is not equivalent to a well-considered appraisal of the theory, the logic, the methods, and the conclusions of the author.

Developing the ability to evaluate reading assignments does not come as easily as the rendering of affective reactions. How, for example, do students, with their greater openness and acceptance of sexuality, decide if Freud, who was writing about repression, has any value for them? It is very easy to dismiss Freud and call him Victorian, sexist, and even a liar.

To learn to make appropriate judgments, to feel competent to perform the task, students usually will require many examples from the instructor. Of course, we expect that the material selected by the instructor is challenging, important, well written, and applicable in many ways to other works and the students' own lives.

CASE STUDY

An LTD group had just finished discussing the chapter on Freud where he distinguishes the manifest and latent dream.

Sharma: I don't see how he knows what those symbols mean. I don't get it. I don't see what he sees. I dream about waterfalls all the time, and I don't think it means what he says it means.

Ken: Yeah, I agree; it just seems weird to me.

Kelly: Wait a second, you guys. Remember what Freud said, and the Professor emphasized this in her lecture. She said that the key to the meaning of the manifest dream was the dreamer's associations. That means to me that the meanings of things can't be determined in advance, but rather that they are to be figured out by the dreamer and the therapist. That is the meaning of the dream work. The work is done by the dreamer who free-associates to things like waterfalls.

Step 8: Evaluation of Group and Individual Performance

For the discussion group to work, this final step is essential, yet it is the step that meets with the most resistance. The task of evaluating one's own performance as well as other members' performances may appear difficult at first, but for the group to be effective some time must be devoted to evaluating the inevitable individual problems and the group process problems. Some group members want to ignore this step. They don't want to confront their problems or those of their peers, and of course, most people do not wish to be confronted. Here are some checkpoints to consider in formulating an evaluation:

1. How well has the group covered the subject? Did the author's key points make sense?
2. What areas of agreement did the group reach? Were differences resolved? Was everyone heard and understood?
3. Were there questions that needed further clarification?
4. What areas of disagreement are there that can or cannot be answered?
5. Who contributed greatly to the discussion? If someone did not contribute, why not?

We suggest that approximately the last 7 minutes of the discussion be devoted to diagnosing and evaluating group and individual mastery of the material. Group members need to be able to say:

- *Who* and *what* helped
- *Who* and *what* were constructive
- *Who* and *what* inhibited the discussion

Individual behaviors that are nonfunctional or disruptive to the overall group process must be confronted and discussed during this evaluation step. Also, supportive and cooperative behavior that enriches and develops critical thinking should be applauded and encouraged.

The process plan allows the group to follow a specialized plan for discussion. How well the group or individual members respond to this plan is crucial in developing high levels of discussion. Thus all group members have the responsibility to share their evaluations of individual and group performances. In the beginning, it may be important to say (without explanation) some of the following:

"I liked it when Joe . . ."
"I felt good when I said . . ."
"I got upset when Peter . . ."
"I admired Jane when she . . ."
"I got nervous when I forgot . . ."

As the group develops, the focus will be more on subgroup formations and conflicts that hinder understanding.

CASE STUDY

One student made the following observation after the sixth session of the LTD.

Jackie: Seems like you older students have a club. Maybe it's because you're married or because you have kids. You're always talking only to each other. I can't identify with your examples. I'm not older, I'm not married, and I don't have kids.

Marilyn: I can't help that; what am I supposed to do?

Lee: I like those examples, and I'm more like you, Jackie, than like them.

Debra: I don't think Jackie means that we have to stop using examples that are important, but rather that we have to realize that the examples may not be relevant to everyone and that maybe, if we asked first, it would show that we have some awareness of others who may be different.

The sharing of her strong feelings was followed up by the leader a few sessions later. She asked Jackie if she still saw the same subgroups.

Jackie: I don't know. Maybe just expressing my feelings changed things or maybe I changed. In any case, I don't feel left out, and I don't feel that the married, older club exists anymore.

Cognitive Domain

It is appropriate here to interject a few words on the relationship between the group process and the cognitive domain. Although the first four steps of the LTD method depend upon and require memory, the following steps move to a new ground. We conceive of these steps as something that goes beyond memory. The discussion here is upon a higher order of questions and analysis, and we think of these last steps of LTD as a higher order of discussion. Those who have taken any courses in education will remember Bloom's categories of thinking, presented in Table 2.2.

Higher order questions and analysis are not repeated from memory or by simple sensory description. Rather, they require abstract thinking. Higher order analysis demands one to go beyond factual

Table 2.2 Bloom's Categories of Thinking

1. Memory: The student recalls or recognizes information.
2. Translation: The student changes information into a different symbolic form or language.
3. Interpretation: The student discovers relationships among fact, generalizations, definitions, values, and skills.
4. Application: The student solves a lifelike problem that requires the identification of the issue and the selection and use of appropriate generalizations and skills.
5. Analysis: The student solves a problem in the light of conscious knowledge of the parts and forms of thinking.
6. Synthesis: The student solves a problem that requires original, creative thinking.
7. Evaluation: The student makes a judgment of good or bad, right or wrong, according to standards he or she designates.

SOURCE: Based on material in Norris M. Sanders, *Classroom Questions: What Kinds?* (New York: Harper & Row, 1966).

or descriptive statements, to generalize, to relate facts in meaningful patterns, to compare and contrast concepts or principles, to make inferences, and to perceive causes and effects. Higher order discussion calls for the discovery of concepts and their relationships rather than simply for their definitions. They prompt one to use ideas rather than just remember old ones.

The key word in higher order discussion is *why*. The question "Why?" requires that the student to go beyond a factual or descriptive answer although it does not necessarily demand more than memory. The question "Why did the Civil War break out?" is merely a factual or descriptive question if the students are expected simply to *repeat what they were told* in a lecture or textbook. That same question would be a higher order question if they were expected to identify the major causes themselves after considering a variety of conditions and events preceding the war. Like a good murder mystery in which one tries to determine "Who done it," the salient feature of higher order questions is that they lead one to actively figure out answers rather than merely remember them.

Everyone brings a different frame of reference to the classroom, based on the sum of knowledge, experiences, and values. Consequently, a higher order statement for one student might be a factual statement for another. For example, asking one student to prove that two triangles are congruent might be asking that person to perform an entirely new mathematical operation or it may be asking simply for a repetition of a well-known operation.

In the LTD process, students must first recall what the author *says*, then they move on to apply what they learned to other situations. This involves analysis and synthesis. Finally, the students learn to evaluate the material. This process thus promotes the development of these higher order critical-thinking skills.

A final word on the Group Process Plan. As we have indicated, the technique should be used appropriately and creatively. In other words the allotment of time to the steps may vary for different groups, subjects, and course goals. Likewise, the steps themselves may be altered to meet course conditions. The process is intended more as a general plan and guide for the instructor and group members; the instructor should assess the nature of the material, the course objectives, and the student members of the group in order to formulate the most appropriate process. It is important, however, that each discussion group member understands and observes any changes.

Thus far we have discussed the step-by-step process by which the LTD group is conducted. Let us now turn to the interpersonal behaviors that underpin a good discussion group.

3 Criteria for Initiation of Learning Through Discussion

Typical students know what to expect in the traditional lecture situation, but have little or no experience with the discussion method. Thus even the most highly motivated students have difficulty, because they have no pattern of a good group and no clear image of the kind of behavior that would contribute to building one. Consequently, what is needed is a conceptual model of what a good group should be, a model that is shared by all group members. We have already introduced the LTD Group Process Plan, which gives the group a model of how it should operate. Here we examine the interpersonal expectations of LTD. For a discussion group to work, members must conform to certain expectations in interpersonal relations. This standard of performance should be kept in mind as students prepare for their group discussions. Likewise, it should be utilized in the evaluation of the group and of the individual students.

Group pressure or cohesiveness can set up "rules for behavior" for the group. Although none of this is written down, it becomes the "accepted way." A warm and friendly group that accepts ideas thoughtfully will encourage more complete and honest participation. A group whose members work together engenders security,

Table 3.1 Criteria for Developing an Effective Discussion Group

1. Group members must regularly attend and come prepared to discuss the material.
2. Group discussion is a cooperative learning experience.
3. Everyone is expected to participate and interact.
4. Group sessions and the task of learning should be enjoyable.
5. The material is adequately and efficiently covered.
6. Evaluation of the group process and individual contribution to the discussion are integral parts of group operation.

with each member knowing what to expect of others and at what levels they operate. They spend less time "feeling each other out" and more time working on the problems at hand. Again, this group-oriented consideration must not obscure, but rather enhance the particular intent of maximizing learning for the individual student. The essential criteria for developing an effective discussion group are presented in Table 3.1.

1. Group Members Must Regularly Attend and Come Prepared to Discuss the Material

To develop a high level of discussion, students not only must show up, but must participate by expressing their understanding of the reading material. Any small group can be rendered ineffectual by the irregular attendance or nonparticipation of group members. Besides problems of continuity, the members who do participate feel resentful at being in a group in which some of the members refuse to uphold their responsibilities. There must be group agreement that members attend regularly and arrive *prepared*.

2. Group Discussion Is a Cooperative Learning Experience

Students who are accustomed to traditional academic styles may unconsciously accept the idea that competitive learning is the only way to succeed. Much grading reinforces this idea. For example, when instructors announce that they grade on the bell-shaped curve, students immediately know that a certain percentage will get an A and a certain percentage an F. Certainly, students worrying about where they will fall on that curve are not going to be very helpful to their classmates. Even in seminars, students endeavor to shine at the expense of their fellow students.

Aggressiveness, attempts to impress, status seeking, and other such competitive behaviors are nonfunctional in the LTD method; they detract from the goal of mastering the subject matter and diminish the evolution of a cohesive group. Asking for help and helping other members understand promote learning. This is the way one student describes behavior that is status seeking, competitive, aggressive, and destructive to the group:

> I recall one discussion during which tension developed among the individuals in the group because it felt as though we were competing against one another. I felt particularly well prepared for the discussion, and it seemed to me that I was dominating the discussion. I was the only male in the group and maybe I was inclined to be more competitive. I remember feeling good about myself for having a lot to say, yet I remember that I was focusing my comments to the leader instead of sponsoring discussion from the rest of the group. I guess I did want the leader to notice and remember that I was "good" for the purposes of my grade, yet I didn't know that it was at the expense of the rest of the group until the last step of the discussion when we were evaluating the job we had done. One of the girls in the group said that she felt that we were competing with each other for grades and that she felt uncomfortable with this when we were supposed to be working together.

3. Everyone Is Expected to Participate and Interact; Participation and Interaction Based Upon a Cooperative Learning Experience is What LTD Is All About

To develop a high level of discussion, students not only must prepare and show up, but must participate by effectively articulating what they think they understand. A group in which only a few members participate is obviously not a good group. Although it is impossible to have participation meted out into absolutely equal shares, all members should participate some of the time. If a student does not come prepared, then he or she may not be getting much from the group, but more important, that student is certainly not contributing anything to the group. Even those who are not prepared can contribute to the group by listening carefully, trying to understand, and engaging in clarifying, questioning, and summarizing. For successful operation, however, LTD needs the contributions of well-prepared and active members.

Activity involves *listening* and talking. In any learning situation, some understand and some don't. In LTD those who don't understand must communicate that they don't understand, and those who do understand must help them gain understanding. In such interaction, even those who understand are learning. As the old saying goes, you never really learn a subject until you try to teach it. Certainly, after clarifying an elusive component to a fellow student, a discussion group member will find it much easier to explain that point on an exam.

Participation is different from interaction. In groups where each member takes a turn reciting from the assignment, little attention is paid to the current speaker, as the other members are more interested in figuring out what they will say than in listening and responding. Hence, there is participation but no interaction; that is, members do not respond or interact with one another.

Sometimes a student may be prepared but wrong in his or her understanding. If the group members have been listening and interacting, they should be able to correct that student. Other students may think they do not comprehend the material, but the group may be able to show them that they do, in fact, understand. In both cases learning has taken place through the interaction of group members.

4. Group Sessions and the Task of Learning Should Be Enjoyable

A friendly, accepting group climate is important in any learning situation, especially in the LTD method, which requires students to reveal their ignorance and confront their fellow students. When there is a climate of acceptance for learning, group learning is enjoyable. Group discussion is not meant to be a grim business. Quite the opposite! The end result of any discussion group should be the creation of a nonthreatening environment wherein learning becomes rewarding, satisfying, and even exciting.

We were all born with curiosity about the world and the way it works. Anyone who's been around toddlers knows what I mean. They optimistically explore their world, wanting to know the why of it all. More often than not, however, our inquisitiveness and zest for new experiences get crushed somewhere along the line, so learning becomes onerous, frightening, and competitive. The LTD method, with honest and constructive feedback, can prevent competitive and destructive learning practices and can help to motivate, nurture, and recognize democratic and intelligent learning.

5. The Material Is Adequately and Efficiently Covered

Learning is accepted as the basis for LTD, and its significance cannot be overestimated. The student's preparation, cooperative interaction, and cognitive skills are the tools by which group members are able to cover the assigned materials adequately and efficiently, and the Group Process Plan provides a procedural guideline that all groups should follow in order to achieve that goal. Although a caring environment is essential, members should take care not to become so enamored with the cohesiveness of the group that the goal of learning becomes obscured.

6. Evaluation of the Group Process and Individual Contribution to the Discussion Are Integral Parts of Group Operation

A good group accepts the inevitability of procedural problems and is willing to evaluate its progress from time to time as needed. The goal of the evaluation isn't to hurt the feelings of others, but to give constructive feedback, be it negative or positive in nature. One of the most difficult tasks for students to perform is the critical evaluation of a fellow student's intellectual performance. Although this may be one of the more emotionally trying steps, evaluation of the group process as well as individual contributions facilitates the grasp of material by encouraging a high level of group interaction. Evaluation allows students to:

1. Express that they are being helped, encouraged, supported, understood, inhibited, frightened, or intimidated by others
2. Discover how they are perceived and evaluated by others as "helping" or "hindering" their peers
3. Enhance group membership by creating and suggesting solutions to the individual and interpersonal problems that all groups develop

Statements That Hinder/Help Group Facilitation

Small groups are unique in their benefits to individuals. Similarly, individual statements are unique in their impact on small groups. In the widely researched Hill Interaction Matrix, William F. Hill (in press) enumerates four distinct "work" categories that emerge during small group interaction: Conventional, Assertive, Speculative, and Confrontive. To be effective members of a small learning group, students must develop an understanding of the different impact and value of each type of statement.

Conventional and Assertive statements are considered prework in that they do not facilitate a deep understanding of issues, topics, persons, or ideas. Conventional statements relate to the general function or purpose of "socializing." No effort is made to get deeply into the subject matter. Some examples are: "Who is playing UCLA tonight?" "How many midterms do you have?" "I love it when it rains in L.A.!" "What are your plans for the weekend?" "This article was hard. The reading took me 3 hours." "I guess I've always been shy, that's why I don't like talking in groups." An excessive amount of socializing statements often indicate that students aren't prepared or don't understand the material. The information and facts are seemingly important, but they do not help the group in achieving their goal of learning. In fact endless, trivial discussion usurps the goal of LTD, which is to have intelligent and analytical discussions. We can spend lots of time discussing where to shop, the food in the dorms, where people come from, and the like. Some of this is necessary . . . but! (Enough said!)

When students don't wish to understand or agree with some point, but want to be heard and want the group to know what they believe, they tend to make Assertive statements. Students may proclaim: "Midterms suck!" "This class attracts nerds!" "Marx was a jerk!" "You expect me to believe that crap about sex that Freud said? Nuts!" Assertive statements are not intended to master the topic; on the contrary, they are usually made to make a personal point about one's beliefs or to defend oneself in an argument, rather than to facilitate trying to discuss the topic in an analytical fashion. We can believe anything, and we can forcefully and aggressively assert these beliefs. We can announce: "Poverty has always been with us, so what is all this complaining about the homeless?" "There is nothing we can do about the grading curve. Professors believe in it." "The world is flat." "The Martians are coming." But beliefs not based on evidence and assertions not based on documentation do not deepen our understanding of a topic.

Speculative and Confrontive statements, in contrast to Conventional and Assertive statements, encourage groups to begin the task of understanding and discussing ideas, theories, concepts, and issues. Speculative and exploratory statements allow the group to face obstacles to understanding by asking questions that require thoughtful review of the material. By asking for help in understanding complex or puzzling material, a student is doing "work" by formulating as a question his or her barrier to comprehension.

When students wish to *understand* some point, process, or problem, they may make Speculative statements such as "Why do you think men are more aggressive than women?" "What causes people to be anti-Semitic?" "Is racism built into all capitalistic societies?" "When does competition get to be destructive?" "Is competition necessary?" "Is T.V. destructive of intelligence?" "How can we reconcile Freud and Marx?"

When students offer their versions of the answers to the Speculative statements, they are also doing "work" in the form of Confrontive statements. Confrontive statements stand as exemplars of learning and teaching. They are the bases for "high" level discussions. Confrontive statements clarify and synthesize the material in a

32   LEARNING THROUGH DISCUSSION

concise and analytical fashion and teach others about ideas, processes, individuals, and groups.

They are made often with a sense of apprehension, because they are personal versions of the truth. As such they can be shot down. You can't argue with someone who believes that "College sucks" or that "The Martians are coming"; you can try and understand why they feel that way, but you will probably not convince them of an alternative view. On the other hand, you can argue with the following:

> I read the best article about delinquency theory. It said that kids aren't different in what they want out of life, but just in the ways they go about getting it. They accept society's goals, but not in the same way.
>
> I don't know if Freud said everything was sexual, but there sure are a lot of symbolic equivalents of sexuality. Did you ever see how some people handle their guns or their cars? I don't see any way to understand their behavior except through Freud. They invest those objects with so much libido. People become nuts about their cars. Sometimes when they get a scratch, it's as if their arm has been broken.

The LTD process is designed to achieve this high level of discussion. To carry out the process, students need to familiarize themselves with the roles described in the following section and attempt to follow them as closely as possible in the group discussions. If they do so, they will see the power of LTD, and their perception of themselves as individuals, as students, and as group members will grow.

4 Group Members' Roles and Skills

At this point students may still express skepticism about the LTD process in general and concern with what they are going to say, how they are going to say it, and what others will think of them. We attempt here to do LTD justice, but in truth a group will not know the magic of LTD until members dedicate themselves to trying it and working at it. LTD is a powerful tool—give it a chance!

Nonproductive behavior such as competing, withdrawing, and dominating are variables to which all members and groups are vulnerable. The personality and role that a group member plays is the result of a particular type of interpersonal need. Some students may have a tendency to use the group unduly to satisfy legitimate interpersonal needs. It is thus important to realize that individual personalities can and will affect the dynamics of the group discussion. For instance, competitive behavior or flirting may be the result of a need to "impress" good-looking people in the group or simply a desire to "show off." All group members have the responsibility to confront and limit nonproductive or inappropriate behavior.

In contrast, productive behavior maximizes the learning potential of both the group and the individual, and these process skills should be encouraged. These important roles and skills are listed in Table 4.1 and discussed in detail below.

Table 4.1 Group Roles and Member Skills

A. Sequence of task roles specific for discussion of a topic:
1. Initiating
2. Giving and asking for information
3. Giving and asking for reactions
4. Restating and giving examples
5. Confronting and reality testing
6. Clarifying, synthesizing, and summarizing
B. Overall task roles required in the LTD method:
7. Gatekeeping and expediting
8. Timekeeping
9. Evaluating and diagnosing

A. Sequence of Task Roles Specific for Discussion of a Topic

1. *Initiating.* Sometimes a group may have trouble getting started or resuming a discussion if a lull falls; each member waits for another to contribute something first. Anyone can get the ball rolling again, but *someone* has to!

2. *Giving and asking for information.* In the LTD method, students are required to state the general message and the ideas contained in the subtopics. In a well-developed group this information will be readily volunteered, but in a beginning group it may have to be solicited. If the members don't share their understanding of the material freely, the discussion will be awkward and stilted.

3. *Giving and asking for reactions.* If a member does share information, other members of the group must respond for learning to take place. In some groups, no interaction takes place; instead, one member states his understanding of the topic, and then the next member states her understanding, and so on in a rotation process. This type of group ritual results in little understanding as others are not really listening, but rather figuring out what they will say when it is their turn to recite. Members should be able to respond to explanations of other members for everyone to get the most out of the discussion.

4. *Restating and giving examples.* In a subtype of the previous role, a group member restates what another has said, thereby providing feedback and a test of whether the member accurately

communicated what he or she intended. The value of giving examples cannot be overemphasized; a good example clarifies for all the meaning of what is being said in a way no amount of elaboration can accomplish.

5. *Confronting and reality testing.* Involved in both 3 and 4 above, one form of reality testing is to restate what someone else has just said. This provides a test of communication and of the correctness of the idea in the message. Misinformation and misstatements must not be allowed to pass unchallenged or learning will not take place. Confronting is thus an important function. Unfortunately, it is also difficult. Suggesting that someone else's statement is inaccurate in some way while maintaining a warm atmosphere conducive to interactive learning requires a skill that the instructor will have to model.

6. *Clarifying, synthesizing, and summarizing.* Even with the simplest material, groups can get into complicated tangles and are, from time to time, in need of someone to clarify. In addition, after a number of restatements of a topic have been made, synthesis is needed. Both clarifying and synthesizing provide closure, as does summarizing, allowing the group to move on to the next item.

B. Overall Task Roles Required in LTD

7. *Gatekeeping and expediting.* One of the most common behaviors in fulfilling the role of gatekeeping and expediting involves attempts to spread participation. A typical gatekeeping remark is, "We haven't heard from Chris; Chris, what do you think about our involvement in Somalia?" Both gatekeeping and expediting are directly connected with moving the group through the group process stages.

8. *Timekeeping.* Time management is of particular importance in the LTD method. If a group is to keep within its time budget, someone must keep an eye on the clock, at least until the group learns to pace itself automatically.

9. *Evaluating and diagnosing.* All members should participate in group evaluation. Even when the evaluation is deferred until the last step in the group process, members need to fill this role silently during the ongoing discussion or else there will be little to bring up.

Nonfunctional Roles

A group may experience both overt and covert resistance to accepting the LTD Process Plan. The point of having a discussion group is to promote learning. Even so, individuals meeting together for an agreed-upon work task can find themselves caught up in a variety of emotional feelings that can hinder or obscure the learning group process.

The following seven role behaviors are types of behavior that emerge in groups and cause difficulties. They are problems, and as such are counterproductive to good discussion. We suggest some remedies that we have found useful.

1. *The silent ones.* An important tenet of LTD is that it be comfortable and possible for everyone to participate. Although *it is not mandatory for each person to verbalize* ideas at every meeting, a person must both listen and verbally participate to be considered a true group member. Silent members are inevitably seen as a "drag," people who don't pull their load. It is mandatory that silent and active members work together to determine the reason behind a member's silence and explore ways in which silent members can become productive.

   a. If silence is caused by lack of knowledge of the subject, members can help by suggesting the silent person be responsible for the author's general statement. This can help start that person on the road to reading and participating. Taking responsibility for the general statement for the next meeting is a first important step.

   b. If silence is caused by confusion as to group process, students can help by defining the LTD step they are discussing or attempting to summarize exactly what members are currently covering. If a student then repeats the last statement or question again, he or she will have brought the whole group to the same point and the discussion can regain its momentum with every member involved.

   c. If silence is caused by not understanding the discussion, a student can help by making requests for questions from the group: "Is this clear, or is there something that any of you wants to question or have clarified?"

   d. If silence is caused by a member's slowness in phrasing his or her thoughts in a quick-talking group, the group should pause for this person. A pause does not have to be filled up immediately. Saying

"Some of us need a little time to think that over" can help the shy or slow person and thus help the entire group.

e. If silence is caused by shyness, the leader can help by asking shy members to speak when they show signs of having something to say. All do not have to compete in the marketplace with those who have stronger voices and quicker reactions. Even if someone else has said it, the "shy" can repeat points in their own words. Some people will not speak unless called on; they will talk only if no one else has anything to say. Others slide in easily on the previous speaker's pause for breath. Neither is "right" nor "wrong," but the discussion leader and individual group members must work to see that both get equal opportunity. (In general it is good advice to leaders and members not to call on others unless they are pretty sure the person won't be embarrassed.)

2. *The overparticipant.* Because our goal is to make everyone comfortable in the group discussion, we have to recognize that just as some are more comfortable with silence, others are uncomfortable unless they verbalize all their thinking. The group's job is to help verbal members to use their facility in a way that is pleasant and productive and helpful for the group. Verbalizing frequently is not necessarily overparticipation, but talk that does not help the group move toward its goal, that leads it in other directions (less profitable ones), that takes too long in relation to the value of the idea to the group, or that makes others very uncomfortable may be considered counterproductive and therefore inhibiting the desired achievement of individual and group learning.

a. *The dominant one* answers questions in a way that seems to quiet all other voices. The leader and members can, in refusing to be awed, ask for other points of view. The leader may attempt to bring in another viewpoint by saying, "That's one side of it; would someone like to comment on how the subjects in the experiment might feel about the view that Susan expressed?"

b. *The repeater* says it once, twice, and then "in other words," again. Individual students can, if they get the gist of it the first or second time, slide in just before the replay starts again, with a brief summary of the point and its relation to the question under discussion. This is not a trick, but more like an aid. Those who repeat themselves usually do so because they feel they have not made themselves clear, so when another person comes in with a neat summary or rephrasing, they are pleased at having their ideas understood by the group.

3. *The wanderer* has the germ of an idea but has not thought it through. Other group members can help such persons by waiting

until the wanderers have expressed enough of the idea to communicate, then coming in with, "Are you saying that . . . ?" or "Do you mean that . . . ?" or "Could you show us how that would work in this situation?" Any of these or other similar questions can help wanderers to clarify in their own mind the thoughts they are trying to express. Once they see the suggested tactic work, they may thereafter decide to wait until they have thought their ideas through before starting in. Thus the group members have helped them test their own ideas.

4. *The tangent person* comes up with, "That just reminded me of so and so," and goes off into a point that is only dimly related to the subject of discussion, or that is related but leads the group into a different aspect of the subject that was not planned for this meeting. Such members may be helped by a question from the group immediately after their comment, which leads the discussion back on track. Or if the relationship to the subject is obscure to the discussion leader, the discussion leader may ask the member to relate it to the subject with a question like, "Do you mean that you think economic sanctions against South Africa must be weighted against the dislocations that boycotts may cause and that you want to know how many people will be put out of work or starve before you support the author's argument for a boycott of South Africa?" In some cases, it is good to let the tangential comment pass with no comment, but inject a summary of where the group is at this point in the discussion. Sometimes a seeming tangent is an important and relevant issue, and if the group seems to wish to pursue it, this should be allowed, as long as the discussion leader tells the group that by so doing they will have to give up some other part of the planned program due to time constraints. This should not be done unhappily, but in the spirit of genuine willingness to abide by the group's choice. If no choice is possible, it should not be offered to the group.

5. *The storyteller.* Personal experience and anecdotes are valuable to a group. Storytellers often make up in warmth and friendship for what they take away from the group in time. Nevertheless, when the stories get too long, or there are too many of them, the discussion leader should say warmly and sincerely that "We wish we had time for all of us to share these experiences, but because of the short-term goal maybe we had better wait for a social hour when we can hear all about . . ."

6. *The insecure talker.* Often the injection of seemingly irrelevant comments or rambling observations is caused by an individual's feeling of insecurity in the group. If all members can be made to feel that they have a place and are really accepted by the others, this kind of "feeling around" for "a place in the sun" can be substantially reduced. This type of participant may be helped by praise for a contribution to the discussion or by being asked to prepare something specific for the next meeting.

7. *The lone dissenter.* An obstinate person expressing a minority voice may seem like a problem if the person is forceful, stubborn, or adamant. But this can become an asset rather than a "problem situation" if the discussion leader helps the group appreciate the voice of dissent and treat it with respect. Comments like, "That really sets me thinking about this in a new way"; "I wonder if we could think along those lines for a moment"; or "That really poses a challenge to the way we've been talking. I'd like to try it on for a moment. Now you're saying that we men are all sexists even if we are androgynous? Tell me why you think I am. Have I acted in any way in this group that indicates to you that you are correct about me or the other males?"

Preparing for Discussion

Very simply, student members must internalize and implement the process plan and play the group roles such as sponsoring and giving encouragement. Most important, they must prepare for discussion meetings. Students should read over the assignment once to get the general sense of it, approaching the material as if they were conducting a silent group meeting, and prepare contributions at each step of the process. A preparation outline is provided in Table 4.2, and the kinds of information to be noted are indicated for each step.

If students follow the preparation outline, they will have learned a great deal before the discussion begins. As the discussion progresses, they may include additional ideas. Thus the outline becomes an excellent source of review for examinations. It is particularly effective to have the preparation sheets handed in at the end

Table 4.2 Outline for Preparation

Step 1: Definition of terms and concepts
List all the words of which you are unsure. Look them up and write down their definitions.

Step 2: Statement of author's message
Write down your version of a general statement of the author's message.

Step 3: Identification of major themes
Identify the subtopics in the article.

Step 4: Discussion of major themes and subtopics
Write out a brief statement of the subject matter of each subtopic. Design a question that you would ask for each.

Step 5: Integration of material with other knowledge
Write down the meaning or usefulness the material has for understanding other concepts. Indicate what other ideas the material substantiates, contradicts, or amplifies.

Step 6: Application of the material
Write down how the material can apply to your own life situations—past, present, or future—or what implications the article has for your own intellectual interests or pursuits.

Step 7: Evaluation of author's presentation
Write down your reactions and evaluation of the assignment.

---

of each class session for the instructor to evaluate and make suitable notes before returning them.

We suggest that the actual book be closed during the group meeting; otherwise members will tend to look through the material, trying to find the answer. If everyone prepares in advance, the discussion will move along with ease and efficiency.

Active Listening Skills

While participating in a group discussion, each student must concentrate on communication skills as well as active listening skills that promote good interaction and learning. The LTD group will have a greater chance of being successful if students learn to be good, active listeners.

We have all been in classes in which the instructor asks a question, only to be greeted by a deafening silence. In an authoritarian, instructor-led group, the instructor usually ends up answering the question, but the LTD method demands that the students both ask the questions and answer them. If members are actively listening, their chances of learning and contributing to the group discussion are greatly improved.

To listen to others and to be successful in understanding them requires empathy. At various times, for various reasons, we all have trouble listening—we "tune out" and "turn off." Although there may be good reasons for tuning out in some situations, we would like group members to adopt a mind-set where they continually struggle to try to understand why they tune out, and to try to listen. The following are things that all of us do some of the time and some of us do all of the time, and that we should all try to do less of the time:

When we *compare* ourselves to others, we tend not to listen.

When we try to *second-guess* what others are saying, we tend not to listen.

When we *rehearse*, we tend not to listen.

When we *judge* people negatively (communist, right-winger, stupid), we tend not to listen.

When we tend to adopt what other people say in order to talk, we tend not to listen.

When we *give advice*, we tend not to listen.

When we *placate* (be nice, always agree, never get involved), we tend not to listen.

Active listening carries a strong element of personal risk: To sense deeply the feelings of others, to understand the meaning their experiences have for them, to see the world as they see it—we risk being changed ourselves. For example, if we permit ourselves to listen our way into the psychological life of fellow students, be they pro-life, or pro-choice, or agitator—to grasp the meaning that their position has for them—we risk coming to see the world as they see it. It is threatening to give up, even momentarily, what we believe and start thinking in someone else's terms. It takes a great deal of inner security and courage to be able to risk ourselves in understanding one another. If group members are only concerned with trying to impress the group and miss hearing dialogue

Table 4.3 Group Maintenance Roles for Members

Group maintenance roles to facilitate group and individual satisfaction:	
1. Encourager	(praises, agrees, accepts others' ideas)
2. Harmonizer	(mediates, relieves tension)
3. Compromiser	(comes halfway, yields status, admits error)
4. Expediter	(encourages and facilitates participation of others)
5. Observer	(records group process, feeds back to group when needed)
6. Evaluator	(commentator evaluation, i.e., "It might be better if we accepted one definition of this term just for the purpose of this discussion; we seem to be bogged down by definitions.")
7. Follower	(goes along with the group, actively accepts its decisions, listens attentively)

that may promote the learning of all the members, then not only will they not learn anything, but this type of inattention to others will have a negative effect on other group members. Everyone should discover his or her own techniques for improving listening, but in general, good listening involves taking the role of others and *accepting* them.

Beyond employing the ability to listen, successful LTD members are committed not only to their own learning but to the group members' learning as well. This is why thorough and in-depth preparation of the assigned material is so imperative. If members have to read an assignment two or three times to truly grasp its details, they should not hesitate in doing so. Not only are they enabling themselves to speak more competently about the given work, but chances are they will bring to other members a higher level of discussion that will in turn foster a higher level of group discussion. The discussion group will be more productive if members share in assuming the seven positive roles listed in Table 4.3, which embody behaviors that help produce high-level discussions.

Finally, group participants have a role similar to the leaders in that they should be able to evaluate the group of which they are members honestly and critically. Rather than viewing the students in a group either as competitors or simply as peers, members should view others as part of a united team, all striving toward the same goal of achieving group cohesiveness and intellectual power.

What we have discussed thus far are roles and behaviors all group members should emulate. In the next chapters we will look at the roles of the group leader and the instructor.

5 Role of the Leader

The student leader guides the group process and may also be responsible for evaluating or grading individual participation. A successful discussion leader must desire the responsibility that accompanies the leader role. Such responsibility includes presenting honest and critical feedback to group members as well as holding the group accountable for following the process method. Leaders need to possess the analytical, cognitive, and interpersonal skills to decipher when a group has fully comprehended the assigned text and if in fact the level of discussion supports an in-depth understanding of the given text.

The instructor may appoint certain students as leaders at the start of the school term or may choose a rotating leadership. In beginning sessions the leaders do not join in on discussion of the material; their main job is to guide group progress within the constructs of the LTD method. They make notes on the group's operation and then "feed back" observations to the group and offer suggestions for overcoming difficulties that the members may be encountering.

As the group becomes more proficient at the LTD process, the leader begins to participate more actively in the group discussion, and should not rescue the group members every time they encounter difficulty. Every member should understand the potential problems and be familiar with suggested solutions. Nevertheless, there will be occasions when the group won't be able to resolve the confusion, and the leader will be called upon to remedy the problem. Obviously, this means that the leader must have a concise and in-depth knowledge of the material to be discussed and some understanding of small group behavior (the instructor may have to guide students in this area).

Instructor-Led Groups

The group leaders have an added responsibility. Prior to each discussion, they are required to meet with the other leaders and the instructor of the course in an instructor-led discussion group, assuming the alternative role of group member. In this instructor-led group, their contributions as individuals and as group participants are critically analyzed and evaluated. They also receive feedback on their performances as leaders, which has been closely scrutinized by the instructor, who sits in on the groups from time to time. Leaders also use their time with the instructor to update problems as well as successes with their group. Thus student leaders are required to prepare not only for the discussion group they facilitate, but also for the group in which they are individually facilitated, demanding a more intensive and thorough degree of academic commitment.

Although students will always instinctively depend on the person designated as in charge, the leader must be someone who can encourage them to—or even insist that they focus and rely on the group for direction and support instead. If in a given group members look to the assigned leader for continual approval and involvement in the discussion, a successful leader will pull back and tighten the boundaries between task and socioemotional dimensions.

Grading

The leader may also serve as the designated "grader" for the group. In this capacity, the leader is responsible for grading the other student members of the group. Because this is a very difficult role to perform, the appointment of any student to the discussion leader role (or grader) must be done with great care. Although not all students are equipped for or desire to assume this specific role, those who do find this to be a challenging and most rewarding position. Variations and modifications of this role can be left to the discretion of individual instructors.

When the student fulfilling the role of leader is responsible for evaluating and grading his or her own peers, the instructor should alleviate much of the accompanying anxiety for the leader as well as for the group members by providing a checklist for the group leader to use to grade performances. The checklist presented in Table 5.1 represents a 10-point scale designating a range from outstanding to unacceptable. Although complete objectivity is never a possibility in any method of grading, whether it be in creating Scantron questions, analyzing essays, or evaluating LTD work, we wholeheartedly believe that this checklist combined with a solid leader reduces the amount of potential subjectivity that might otherwise be employed.

Student-Leader Grading Guidelines

1. Leaders/graders should provide students with their grades after every few discussion sections. This is best done by handing out individual slips of paper with grades and dates. In this way, members will know how they are doing and will be able to ask why they received a less-than-satisfactory grade. They will also have time to work to improve their group participation before final grades are assigned.

2. Leaders should adhere to the grading standards without deviation. On occasion the instructor will ask to see the grades and compare them with his or her observations.

3. Leaders should never lead groups containing close friends, roommates, or romantic interests.

4. Leaders are expected to discuss with the instructor all difficulties they are having with their groups.

5. Leaders are expected to compile a list of members' names and telephone numbers at the first meeting and provide a copy for all members at the second meeting. As a result, members will have the

Table 5.1 The LTD Grading Checklist

Use a 10-point scale. This is very important.

A+ is 10. This is for outstanding work.

A = 9.5, B = 8.5, C = 7.5. Thus,

A– to A+ corresponds to 9.0 - 10, and anything in between is in the A range.

B– to B+ corresponds to 8.0 - 9.0 . . . and so on. You can use 8.0, 8.1, 8.2, 8.3, etc.

A Represents very excellent work. Students use group to help deepen, extend, and integrate their own and others' work. Integrations must teach others, must be informed. They are not stories.

B Represents solid, respectable work. Knows work but doesn't see extensions, implications. Student is accurate in reporting and detailing author's message.

C Stands for work that is O.K.; student knows the work but not with clarity or depth. Knows general message. Misses details and subtleties. Not really on top of material.

D Is barely passing. Only a glimmer of knowledge is there.

F Is a fail! If absent, a student gets a –, and if there's no participation, then the student receives a 5.0.

---

resources necessary to call one another if they encounter difficulty with the reading or any other aspect of the LTD process.

Some students—and some instructors—may still have reservations about student graders. However, we have found that most student leaders, under the guidance of the instructor, are diligent in fulfilling their role.

6 Role of the Instructor

The following are the beliefs and guidelines developed over the many years that we have used this method and for which the instructor plays a unique and paramount role. First, because the quality of learning is obviously limited by the quality of the materials used, the instructor must select materials that are deep, interesting, and worthy of discussion. We cannot stress this enough. No matter how good the individual group members are, the discussion groups will not live up to their potential if the course materials are deficient. If there is no adequate text in the field, the instructor must write out and copy any lecture notes or journal articles and make them available to students in advance.

Resource Expert

During class periods, instructors must assume the role of resource expert. Although they should not rescue the group every time members encounter difficulty, on occasion group members will not have the background to resolve their confusion and the text may not be of much help. Serving as a resource expert is more difficult in large classes that are broken down into several small discussion groups. In this case, the instructor should either circulate

from group to group or hold meetings of the entire class once a week
at which questions raised in group discussions can be covered.

Group Trainer

Another role that the instructor plays is that of group trainer.
Because of unfamiliarity with the Learning Through Discussion
method, students need help in understanding the goals of the
discussion groups, the process involved, and the roles they must
perform. As mentioned previously, the instructor may wish to
hold an LTD group during the first class meeting or play the video
Learning Through Discussion so that students can see the process
being played out. Once the groups are successfully launched, the
instructor should observe how each group is progressing and offer
suggestions for overcoming difficulties that arise.

The instructor may also wish to appoint a process observer who
makes notes on the group operations while abstaining from the
discussion. The process observer then makes a brief report to the
total group. This should be a temporary position so the person can
spend time as a functioning part of the group. Moreover, once the
group is functioning fully, there will be little need for a process
observer; rather the individual members should be able to discern
any problems.

After the students have had a chance to read this book (we
recommend by the second meeting), the instructor will need to
select group leaders. We have found that asking for volunteers
works very well, although some instructors may wish to appoint
leaders, either for the entire semester or on a rotating basis.

Resource for Group Leaders

In addition to the above responsibilities, the instructor must be
both the trainer and resource for the group leaders. Despite their
intelligence and natural leadership skills, the student group leaders
need the instructor's knowledge and support. They are encountering unknown territory and may find it uncomfortable at times.

They will also need help with the substantive materials, so contact with them on an ongoing basis is extremely important.

Ideally, five to eight leaders can evaluate 30-64 students. For larger classes we have used 12-16 leaders, dividing them into two groups. The instructor can meet with one group while the other meets alone or with a teaching assistant. Or, the groups can be divided into an inner circle and an outer circle. The inner circle discusses and the outer circle evaluates. Most important to the entire method is the instructor's belief in the value of this form of learning; with that firmly in place even large classes can benefit from LTD.

The instructor needs to meet with the group leaders for the same amount of time that the student leaders meet with their groups, preferably right before the student-led groups meet. Because they will be using the instructor as a model of LTD leadership, he or she needs to show them how to go through all the steps, how to spend time on evaluation, and how to encourage constructive criticism. In the meetings with the group leaders, the instructor must use time carefully and prudently and follow the schedule that the leaders will subsequently follow in their group.

The instructor needs to help the leaders understand that all LTD groups are different from one another. Their self-led groups will be different from instructor-led groups. Indeed they, themselves, will help shape their group. For example, some leaders will have favorite steps as well as problems with other aspects of the method. Some leaders will love applications, others will dislike vocabulary. Helping leaders visualize these truths may require the instructor to discuss the dynamics of small group behavior with them.

Student Grading

Student leaders, unaccustomed to grading their peers, will also need help separating objective evaluation criteria from like or dislike of individual students. The instructor must help the leaders understand that their individual problems with students are really group problems that impede the group's success and therefore must be solved by the group. We recommend that the instructor visit the groups to provide guidance to both the leaders and the members and to pinpoint problems that the groups might overlook.

An instructor may also want to consider employing the LTD Preparation Exercise we have created or the following alternative grading system suggested by Jina Yoon.

In the true LTD spirit of "democratic participation," we suggest implementing a grading system in which the students themselves take an active role. This system involves asking students to evaluate critically their own and others' performances at the end of each session. Students often have a difficult time with the idea of assessing the work of others, much less their own, and because of this, many of them may feel uncomfortable or unprepared to take on the task of critical evaluation. For this reason, we suggest that students be given the option to use either the previously described grading system in which the leader is solely responsible for the students' grades or one in which the leader and the students are equally responsible. To best implement the latter method, you may choose to pass out confidential evaluation forms in the last few minutes of each discussion period. To reduce the potential for subjectivity, these forms may contain the following objective evaluative criteria and corresponding scales for each:

STUDENT'S GRASP OF WRITTEN MATERIAL
Poor 1. . . . 2. . . . 3. . . . 4. . . . 5. . . . 6. . . . 7. . . . 8. . . . 9. . . . 10 Excellent

STUDENT'S ABILITY TO ARTICULATE VERBALLY HIS OR HER THOUGHTS
Poor 1. . . . 2. . . . 3. . . . 4. . . . 5. . . . 6. . . . 7. . . . 8. . . . 9. . . . 10 Excellent

STUDENT'S ABILITY TO APPLY AND EXTEND THE MATERIAL
Poor 1. . . . 2. . . . 3. . . . 4. . . . 5. . . . 6. . . . 7. . . . 8. . . . 9. . . . 10 Excellent

STUDENT'S OVERALL CONTRIBUTION TO GROUP LEARNING
Poor 1. . . . 2. . . . 3. . . . 4. . . . 5. . . . 6. . . . 7. . . . 8. . . . 9. . . . 10 Excellent

Whatever method of grading is selected as most appropriate within the framework of a specific course, leaders need to understand grading standards. The instructor must ensure that the students receive feedback grades on a regular basis throughout the course term.

Final Suggestions

Instructors should approach the training creatively, devising their own variations of the method and experimenting with different approaches in order to improve it. Below are some adaptations made by previous instructors that may be of some help.

1. In introducing the class, a brief explanation of the need for structure and the three parts of LTD is necessary. Further, many instructors require that all participants acquire a copy of this book and read it prior to the first regularly scheduled discussion session.

2. The instructor may conduct a demonstration group in which he or she assumes responsibility for moving the group through the LTD process steps.

3. Initial meetings might deal with easier material that the group could practice on.

4. A rule should make it permissible to consult the text only for points of fact. Otherwise, the text should remain closed during the class discussion so students do not bury themselves in it instead of interacting with other group members.

5. Some sort of postmeeting reaction sheet on which students check or otherwise indicate their reactions and evaluations of group meetings can be useful (see Appendix). These can be tallied by the group leader and the results given to the group. When these are accumulated so that the group can see how the ratings have shifted over a span of several meetings, this often leads to some insightful discussions of the group and its problems.

6. One final word to the instructor: The LTD method will work only if you are firm in your demand that the group follow the method.

A Last Word

If the instructor and students give LTD a chance to demonstrate its special nature and value, we believe that you will all see that students become more able and competent in formulating sound verbal arguments, understanding issues of complexity in greater depth, and self-exploration as a way to understand ideas. In addition, students will develop a greater appreciation of themselves as teachers and learners and the potential of their peers as teachers. These beliefs will help facilitate a stronger commitment to lifelong learning. In sum, LTD often works to reduce student alienation from higher learning. Endless educational possibilities await students at LTD's front door. It is our hope that those already well acquainted with the LTD method and those just learning about it for the first time will thrive intellectually and feel personally empowered using the LTD process.

We welcome hearing from all instructors and students about their LTD experiences. We know that many will modify and adopt the LTD structure to their own setting. One student in Professor Rabow's social psychology class reported that her Bible class had adopted the LTD method. Although this was certainly an unanticipated consequence of her learning the method and becoming more interested in learning, it does point to the ways in which learning can be revitalized and democratized.

Appendix

Skills Useful for Classroom Discussion

Before the Discussion

Preparation

a. With a copy of the discussion outline before you, as you read, jot down ideas wherever you think they fit best into the discussion.

b. Look up and learn to say the meanings of new words and concepts.

c. When you have finished reading, go back through the outline and write down reminders of what you might say during each step in the discussion.

d. Practice saying or formulating questions about material you anticipate introducing into the discussion.

During the Discussion

Step 1—Definition of terms and concepts

a. List the words or concepts with which you had some difficulty and ask others to add to your list.
b. Try to define or explain one of the words on your list.
c. Ask the group members if you have defined it as they understand it.
d. Encourage others to practice explaining what it means to them.
e. Restate what someone else has said to make sure you understand it.
f. Give an example to clarify the meaning.
g. Ask the group members if everyone understands the new words or concepts.

Step 2—Statement of the author's message

a. State in your own words what you think the assignment was all about.
b. Frame a question that will encourage someone else to state what the assignment was about.
c. Encourage other group members to practice explaining it.
d. State the ways in which your understanding or interpretation differs from that stated by another member.
e. Ask for clarification on points you don't understand.
f. Restate what someone else has said if you need to, to be sure you know it.
g. If you think two other members are misunderstanding each other, try to lessen the confusion.

Step 3—Identification of major themes

a. Note organization of author's material in terms of headings and subheadings used.
b. Consider what makes for a logical sequence of subtopics.

Step 4—Discussion of major themes and subtopics

a. Ask the group to state the essential elements of the author's presentation.
b. Practice saying for yourself what the author was mainly concerned with and encourage others to do so.

Step 5—Integration of material with other knowledge

a. State the meaning or usefulness of the new material in understanding other ideas or concepts.
b. Phrase questions that will stimulate group members to see how the new material fits into what they have studied previously.
c. Ask or state how the new material contradicts, substantiates, or amplifies some previously developed point.
d. Summarize into compact statements points others have made.
e. Listen critically for and try to state puzzling aspects of the material that are giving the group trouble.
f. Ask for or give help in stating the material more concisely.
g. Call the group's attention to and reinforce a comment that seems particularly helpful.

Step 6—Application of the material to self

a. Ask or state why and how the new material can be useful to members.
b. Give examples of how you might apply it or how the knowledge of it may be useful to you.
c. Compare to your own experience the author's reasons for thinking it worthwhile.
d. Test the usefulness of the new material by constructing a situation for which it could be useful.
e. Give examples you know of that the new material helps to explain or helps you to understand.

Step 7—Evaluation of author's presentation

a. Pose questions to help the group evaluate the new material, the method of arriving at the conclusions, etc.
b. State points supporting or questioning the validity of the arguments or the reasoning of the author.
c. State why and how you think the new material is or is not useful.
d. Frame questions that will help the group to test the usefulness of specific points.

Postmeeting Reaction Sheets (PMRS)

I. Reactions to Group Meeting

Name: _____

Date: _____

Instructions: Mark an X on the line above your response to the following questions.

1. I felt that the group meeting today was:

| Excellent | Good | Average | Not So Good | Bad |

2. I felt that my participation in the group was:

| Very Good | Good | Average | Not Very Good | Bad |

3. My feelings during the meeting were mainly:

| Very Enjoyable | Pleasant | So-So | Unpleasant | Quite Unpleasant |

4. I felt that I learned from the discussion:

| Very Much | Quite a Bit | Some | Little | Not at All |

Remarks:

II. Execution of Cognitive Map

Instructions: For each step of the Cognitive Map, indicate your rating of how the group performed the step by placing a check mark in one of the five boxes.

RATINGS

Steps in the Cognitive Map	1 Very Good	2 Quite Adequate	3 Fairly Good	4 Not So Good	5 Poorly
1. Definition of Terms					
2. General Statement					
3. Subtopic Designation					
4. Subtopic Discussion					
5. Integration					
6. Application					
7. Evaluation					

III. Member Roles Inventory

Instructions: Please indicate which of the following roles you played some of the time today by making check marks in the A column opposite the roles you played.

Please indicate which of the following roles you felt were exercised adequately by the group today by making check marks in the B column opposite those roles which were played.

Positive Roles

A	B	
		Initiating
		Gave information
		Asked for information
		Gave positive reactions or opinions
		Gave negative reactions or opinions
		Asked for positive reactions or opinions
		Asked for negative reactions or opinions
		Gave confrontation or reality tested
		Gave restatement of others' contributions
		Asked for restatement of others' contributions

A	B	
		Gave examples
		Asked for examples
		Gave clarification, synthesis, or summary
		Gave comment on group's movement or lack of it
		Asked for comment on group's movement or lack of it
		Sponsored, encouraged, helped, or rewarded others
		Standard setting
		Physical movement of objects
		Relieved group tension

Negative Roles

A	B	
		Acted with aggressiveness and hostility
		Made self-confessions
		Acted with defensiveness
		Was competitive
		Withdrew

A	B	
		Sought sympathy
		Pleaded for a pet idea
		Horsed around
		Was dominating
		Did some status seeking

60

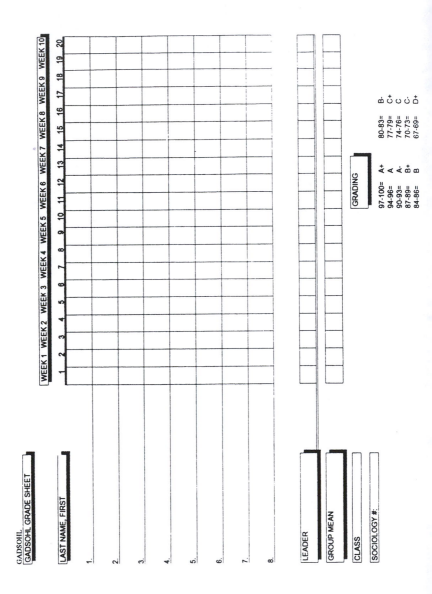

GADSOHL
GADSOHL GRADE SHEET

LAST NAME, FIRST

1.
2.
3.
4.
5.
6.
7.
8.

	WEEK 1	WEEK 2	WEEK 3	WEEK 4	WEEK 5	WEEK 6	WEEK 7	WEEK 8	WEEK 9	WEEK 10
	1 2	3 4	5 6	7 8	9 10	11 12	13 14	15 16	17 18	19 20

LEADER

GROUP MEAN

CLASS

SOCIOLOGY #:

GRADING

97-100= A+
94-96= A
90-93= A-
87-89= B+
84-86= B
80-83= B-
77-79= C+
74-76= C
70-73= C-
67-69= D+

LTD Evaluation Form

Name _____

Class _____

Instructor _____

Subgroup _____

You are being asked to complete this questionnaire in order to evaluate systematically the Learning Through Discussion method. Your evaluation will be kept confidential so that your instructor will not be able to identify individual responses.

Please circle the response that most closely reflects your feelings.

1. Was this your first experience in a discussion group class?
   a. yes   b. no

2. Have you previously had a course using the LTD method?
   a. yes   b. no

3. What was your initial reaction to the LTD method?
   a. enthusiastic   b. sounded O.K.
   c. wait and see   d. slightly negative
   e. negative

4. Were you aware that the LTD method was to be used when you signed up for the class?
   a. yes   b. no

5. Do you feel that the method used was appropriate for the subject matter?
   a. yes   b. partly
   c. no

6. Do you feel that the instructor adequately supported and implemented the LTD method?
   a. yes   b. no

7. How much time did the instructor spend in your discussion group?
   a. not at all   b. very little
   c. occasional visits   d. frequent visits contributing
                                      meaningfully to the group
                                      discussion

8. What determined your grade?

a. tests

b. peer evaluation

c. preparation sheets

d. a combination of a, b, and c (specify)

9. In your experience has the LTD method been useful in the mastery of material that otherwise would have been difficult?

a. yes

b. no

10. Do you feel that you grasped a real understanding of the basic facts of what the author had to say on the subject?

a. yes

b. partly

c. no

11. In your opinion did the group cognitive map lessen the amount of time spent on useless argument?

a. yes

b. no

12. Was the definition of terms and concepts helpful in group communication?

a. yes

b. somewhat

c. no

13. Did your discussion group apply itself according to the time limit set by the group?

a. yes

b. sometimes

c. no

14. Do you think your ability to think critically was enhanced by the LTD method?

a. yes

b. somewhat

c. no

15. In your group was there a prevalence of a warm, accepting, nonthreatening climate?

a. yes

b. no

16. Did you feel you were competitive toward other members?

a. yes

b. no

17. How would you rate the level of interaction in your group?

a. high

b. medium

c. low

18. Were the leadership functions adequately distributed?

a. yes

b. no

19. In your opinion were the members effective as group leaders?

a. yes

b. no

20. Did the group session make the learning task more enjoyable for you?
    a. yes   b. no

21. Was the subject matter in the book adequately and efficiently covered?
    a. yes   b. no

22. How many members did not attend regularly?
    a. everyone   b. nearly everyone
    c. about half   d. a few
    e. practically none

23. How many members usually did not come prepared?
    a. everyone   b. nearly everyone
    c. about half   d. a few
    e. practically none

24. Do you feel that your participation in the method has changed the way you feel about other people?
    a. yes   b. somewhat
    c. no

25. Do you feel that your participation has changed the way you feel about yourself?
    a. yes   b. somewhat
    c. no

26. If the occasion should arise, would you ever use the LTD method in teaching or administration?
    a. yes   b. no

Discussion Questions

A. Are there any ways in which you would like to see the LTD method changed? If so do you have any suggestions for alternatives?

B. What do you see as the major advantages of the LTD method as compared to the lecture method?

Research on the LTD Method

LTD has been used all over the country by many instructors in a variety of courses. Both Professors William Hill and Jerome Rabow have used it successfully in courses in sociology, psychology, social psychology, statistics, and research methodology at different universities and in different countries. Many unsolicited letters from instructors and students who report success and satisfaction with the LTD method have been mailed to Sage.

The value of *Learning Through Discussion* cannot rest merely on testimonials, anecdotal evidence, or case studies but lies in systematic research that might establish the benefits of the method in contrast to other teaching methods. While there is no well-established body of empirical materials, there are few well-conducted studies that are favorable to the LTD method. The shortage of materials is due in part to the need to have a valid comparison between lectures and discussions. We believe that students in lectures tend to focus on thinking about and committing facts to memory, while students using the LTD method focus upon developing skills for manipulating ideas. If this is true, research must address both dimensions of learning. Research should reveal that the different methods would produce different results. Objective exams would favor the lecture methodology while essay exams would favor discussion groups. And this is partly what has been found. Before we examine the specific research on LTD, it would probably be beneficial to place LTD in two larger contexts: the context of cooperation in education and the context of education theory.

LTD is above all a cooperative learning method and thus stands in contrast to the individualism and competition that are part of western educational culture. Can cooperation in classrooms work? First, at a general level, there is evidence that cooperative group life is a more stable strategy in evolutionary terms than competition and individualism (Axelrod & Hamilton, 1981). It is also clear that groups form when individuals recogize that they can accomplish a desired goal more successfully or with more enjoyment if they work together. Indeed countries vary in their emphasis upon individualism (one's own personal needs, interests, and goals) and collectivism (group needs, interests, and goals). In Japan, groups are used for doing things that most Americans do alone: for example, going to work and performing calisthenics. Zander puts its simply: "The people of Japan like to do things in groups" (1983, p. 3). While it is often believed that individual competition achieves excellence, it is also true that cooperative groups raise the achievements of members more than competitive groups (Blau, 1954). Moreover, cooperatively structured groups in primary-level public schools have reduced prejudice among students, a goal to which we subscribe. This jigsaw method (Aronson, Stephan, Sikes, Blaney, & Snapp, 1978) is similar to the LTD method in that both methods require students to learn from each other and achieve greater learning. Brewer and Miller (1984) believe that the positive effects of cooperation are enhanced when the group can set limits on the individual's capacity to categorize other individuals. This categorization is broken down by the atmosphere of a small group learning community where individuals are recognized for who they are and what they can contribute. It is these two processes of learning from others and reducing categorization that help increase cooperation and learning in LTD. In LTD, each member's applications and integrations help others learn about themselves and the other members.

What about the context of education? Many educational theorists have recognized the limits of the traditional lecture method. Freire, Ashton-Warner, Holt, and Kozol all offer brilliant analyses of what is wrong with modern public education.

Instructors who are considering adoption of *Learning Through Discussion* undoubtedly feel that they are taking some risk. It is not part of the educational experience to trust students, to bring cooperation into a classroom, and to run the class more democratically. But for those of you who are considering adopting this method, you need not feel that you are alone concerning your fears and your desires and wishes for deeper learning by students. More and more educators are trying to revamp traditional methods. Valerie Bentz (1992) described a learning process at the graduate level that she describes as deep learning. She emphasizes how such learning groups are derived from the theories of Jurgen Habermas, Robert Langs, and Virginia Satir.

In further justification of the method that goes beyond the empirical data, the *Learning Through Discussion* method can be seen as emphasizing a set of goals and values that have been explicated by major educational theorists. William Perry (1970) and Bernard Bloom (1956) have examined the intellectual development and educational objectives that can help us in placing LTD in a larger learning context. Achieving an awareness of the larger deep learning context is essential for the instructor's appointed LTD group discussion leaders. The LTD experience is enhanced by acquainting the leaders with Perry's scheme and Bloom's work explaining the stages as they relate to the diverse mix of undergraduates these leaders should expect to encounter.

The first effort to demonstrate the effectiveness of LTD was conducted by Hill at Idaho State University. Dr. Hill and Dr. Shanna McGee each taught a section of introductory psychology, the former using LTD and the latter lecturing. In the following quarter, the study was replicated, but the roles were reversed: Dr. McGee used the LTD, and Dr. Hill lectured. The same multiple-choice objective questions were used in all four classes. There were no significant differences in mid-term grades obtained between the two types of instruction regardless of which instructor used discussions or lectures. On the final exam, however, the LTD-instructed students were superior. At a subjective level, it was found that most students exposed to LTD reported that they would use the method if they were to teach a similar course. As no essays were required, this study does not establish the superiority of LTD for critical thinking.

In a study conducted by Downs (1972), a number of classes conducted by different instructors at California State Polytechnic University, Pomona, were involved in using the LTD, and the students were required to evaluate their experience on an LTD Evaluation Form. Analysis of these data indicated that a very high proportion of the students rated their LTD experience as very good or excellent overall, and only a small minority rated it as a negative experience. While gratifying and suggestive, there were large variations in the satisfaction levels. Since some instructors got higher ratings than others, and there was variation from class to class or course to course, many questions remained.

As a consequence, the Innovation in the Instructional Process grant was obtained from the Chancellor's Office of the California State Universities to further understanding of the LTD method. The results of this more complicated study may be condensed as follows:

1. *The choice of a text is critical!* The more technical the text, the less satisfaction was expressed with the LTD experience. The texts in engineering and the transformational grammar in English were associated with lower satisfaction scores. Educators have long claimed that the single most important act of the instructor lies in the selection of the text. This remains important for the success of the LTD method.

2. *Students with an interpersonal orientation tend to do better!* The HIM-B *Matrix Form* or interpersonal scores (Hill, 1969) of the engineering students were much lower than those of the humanities and social science students. This is interpreted as meaning they were less open to and sophisticated about small group situations. As a result of these differences, ratings on the PMRs of the group meetings were lower, and as was their overall satisfaction with the LTD experience. The lower ratings were not disastrous, and the instructors felt that with a more appropriate text and with beginning engineering students, the method had much promise.

3. *Group composition matters!* For certain courses in the study, group composition was experimentally varied, and members were placed in discussion groups according to their HIM-B or interpersonal scores. Five different types of groups were thus composed:
   a. All members had high interpersonal scores.
   b. All members had medium interpersonal scores.
   c. All members had low interpersonal scores.
   d. Group had high, medium, and low interpersonal scores.
   e. Group had medium and low interpersonal scores.

The results were very clear. The highly interpersonal groups were positive in their PMRs and the evaluation scores, and the least interpersonal groups were least positive. Thus, to optimize LTD, it is perhaps necessary to exclude the students who have a traumatized approach to group situations and presumed reluctance to participate. This is, of course, not ordinarily possible, and the instructor has to accept and teach the students who enroll in his or her class. It is important to note that both the low group and the medium and low group (c and e) do less well, but the group that has high, medium, and low does quite well. This means that if the instructor can avoid having all low and medium students in the discussion groups and have some high interpersonal types in each group, a satisfactory result can be anticipated.

In a more revealing study, Beilin and Rabow (1979) divided one large sociology class (350 students) into different smaller learning groups—some of which met as LTD groups while the remainder of the students met with their teaching assistants twice a week in groups of 50 students where no focused discussions took place. A final essay exam, consisting of both objective/short-answer and narrative questions, was administered to all students. Students' identities were concealed through the use of their university identification numbers. While there was no reason to believe that the LTD students would do less well on the objective exam, they could be expected to be equally as motivated as the other students. We predicted that the LTD experience would result in higher essay scores. As expected, the results of the exams revealed no significant differences between LTD groups and T. A. groups on the objective and short-answer portions of the exam. However, the results of the narrative portion of the exam showed the essays of the LTD students received higher grades. Since the LTD method stresses a deeper type of learning incorporating analysis, synthesis, and applications, we felt that this research corroborated the value of the LTD group method of learning.

References

Aronson, E., Stephan, C., Sikes, J., Blaney, N., & Snapp, M. (1978). *The jigsaw classroom*. Beverly Hills, CA: Sage.

Axelrod, R., & Hamilton, W. D. (1981). The evolution of cooperation. *Science, 211*, 1390-1396.

Beilin, R., & Rabow, J. (1979). *Development of critical abilities through structural learning groups*. Fifth International Conference on Improving University Teaching, London, England, Conference Papers, pp. 656-659.

Bentz, V. M. (1992). Deep learning groups: Combining emotional and intellectual learing. The Fielding Institute, University of California, Santa Barbara, Texas Women's University, *Clinical Sociology Review*, pp. 71-89.

Bloom, B. S., et al. (1956). *Taxonomy of Educational Objectives: Cognitive Domain*. New York: David McKay.

Brewer, M. B., & Miller, N. (1984). Beyond the contact hypothesis: Theoretical perspectives on desegregation. In N. Miller & M. B. Brewer (Eds.), *Groups in Contact: The Psychology of desegregation* (pp. 281-302). New York: Academic.

Craik, F. I. M., & Lockhart, R. S. (1972). Levels of processing: A framework for memory research. *Journal of Verbal Learning and Verbal Behavior, 12*, 599-607.

Downs, P. (1972). *Study of discussion groups*. Unpublished senior project, California State Polytechnic University, Pomona.

Gutzmer, W. H., & Hill, W. F. (1973). Evaluation of the effectiveness of the learning through discussion method. *Small Group Behavior, 4*(1).

Hill, W. F. (1969). *Hill interaction matrix (HIM) supplement*. Claremont, CA.

Hill, W. F. (1973-1974). Optimizing effectiveness of the discussion method. Pilot project for innovation in the instruction process. Grant funded by the office of the Chancellor, The California State Universities and Colleges.

Hill, W. F. (in press). *Hill interaction matrix: Monograph and scoring manual* (revised). Upland, CA: Howdah Press.

Hill, W. F., Stoller, F. H., & Straub, C. (1967). Group therapy for social impact. *American Behavioral Scientist, 11*(1).

Perry, W. (1970). *Intellectual and ethical development in the college years*. New York: Holt, Rinehart, Winston.

Zander, A. (1983). The value of belonging to a group in Japan. *Small Group Behavior, 14*, 3-14.

About the Authors

Michelle A. Charness graduated from UCLA with honors in sociology and is currently finishing her law degree at Loyola Law School in Los Angeles. She is interested in women's and children's rights and has published on money and gender.

Johanna (Gia) Kipperman graduated from UCLA with a bachelor's degree in sociology / social psychology. She earned a J.D. from Boston University School of Law and currently practices in San Jose, California.

Susan Radcliffe-Vasile did her undergraduate work at UCLA, where she is currently a Ph.D. candidate in the Department of Sociology. Her area of affiliation is in communities and institutions. Her primary research interests reside in applied health care and educational research, mixed cultural identify, and African-American studies. She is a recent recipient of the Presidential Dissertation Fellowship Award. She is also currently employed as a Graduate Mentor for UCLA's Academic Advancement Program. In this capacity, she mentors under-represented students admitted into graduate school. She was an administrator for various South-Central Los Angeles area health and social welfare agencies. In this capacity, she was responsible for designing social welfare programs that serviced the educational and health care needs of community residents.

Jerome Rabow is a Professor of Sociology at UCLA, where he offers courses in social psychology, psychoanalytic sociology, and education. Professor Rabow is also a therapist in private practice in Los Angeles. While he has published more than 100 papers, his research interests, in the past few years, have included drunk-driving intervention, money and gender, and peace. He is also a long-distance runner and a road biker.